The BMW 2002
The *real* story behind the legend

ID Media LLC
Portland, Oregon, USA

Text copyright ©2019 by Jacqueline Jouret
Design copyright ©2019 by Jacqueline Jouret
Photos courtesy BMW AG, the BMW Archive, the BMW Design Archive, Daimler-Chrysler AG

First published in the United States of America in 2019
by ID Media LLC

All rights reserved. No part of this book may be reproduced electronically or mechanically or transmitted online—including photocopies, recordings, or by any electronic storage and retrieval system—without express written permission from the publisher.
Some of the material in this book was published in 2018 by the BMW CCA Foundation in *The ICON: 50 Years of the BMW 2002*, written by Jackie Jouret.

Printed in the United States of America

ISBN 978-1-7333878-0-4

Typeset in Avenir

ID Media LLC
PO Box 10800
Portland, OR 97296 USA

The BMW 2002
The *real* story behind the legend

by Jackie Jouret

Table of Contents

The birth of a modern classic **9**

The 2002's automotive DNA **11**

"Niche Paul" creates a new one **23**

The 1600-2 slots in **31**

The Max factor **37**

The real origins of the 2002 **45**

Type 114…or E10? **53**

BMW drops the Whispering Bomb **57**

Baur builds a cabrio **67**

TI and tii: More is never enough **73**

The Touring experiment **79**

The battery-powered Pacesetter **87**

Toward a Type 114 successor **91**

Square taillights and big bumpers **97**

Edition L, for Luxury **101**

Turbo power for the '02 **103**

Lutz takes on Hoffman **111**

In the end, a new beginning **121**

Appendix: Type 114 exports to US, 1966-'76 **127**

Bibliography **128**

Author's note **129**

Index **130**

The birth of a modern classic

Fifty-one years after its introduction, the 2002 remains the quintessential BMW, embodying the agile handling, just-right performance, and practicality that have been characteristic of the marque since the 1930s. The 2002's tactile feedback is legendary, as is its everyday usability. It's no wonder this compact two-door became wildly popular in the US when new, introducing a generation of American car enthusiasts to a once-obscure Bavarian import. Nor is it a surprise that the 2002 became a modern classic, with well-kept originals and impeccably restored '02s commanding impressive prices.

The 2002's virtues are well known. By contrast, the story of how the 2002 came to be remains mired in misinformation.

Eager to claim credit for the 2002's success, BMW's US importer Max Hoffman insisted the car was his idea. As records within the BMW Archive reveal, it simply wasn't true.

Instead, the car has its origins in BMW's need to build a car that could meet stringent new US emissions regulations, and that could also race competitively in the European Touring Car Championships.

That car became the 2002, which transformed BMW from an obscure Bavarian carmaker into a global success, and ultimately one of the world's most respected corporations. Max Hoffman played a role in that story, certainly, but he wasn't its hero.

No car is the product of one man, and the 2002 was created by a team of passionate engineers, designers, and executives, all of whom labored mightily, on a minuscule budget, to create a car that would live up to the promise of the BMW roundel on its hood.

This is their story.

The 2002's automotive DNA

To understand what made the 2002 a quintessential BMW, we have to begin with the 303 (**opposite**), BMW's first all-new car of its own design.

Bavarian Motor Works is known today as a manufacturer of automobiles and motorcycles, but it began as a builder of aero engines. As such, BMW was part of the aircraft industry that sprang up just prior to World War I around the Oberwiesenfeld military base in Munich, capital of the still-independent kingdom of Bavaria within the German *Reich* (empire) led by Prussia.

BMW's inline six-cylinder IIIa aero engine, introduced in 1917, was considered Germany's finest, and it was the preferred powerplant of *Luftwaffe* pilots. Uniquely effective at high altitudes, the IIIa gave the Germans a distinct advantage in aerial combat. The IIIa arrived too late, however, to change the course of the war which ended in 1918 with Germany's defeat. In the aftermath, BMW lost its lucrative military contracts, then the ability to build airplane engines altogether following restrictions imposed by the Treaty of Versailles in 1919. That led principal shareholder Camillo Castiglioni to diversify BMW's operations by adding motorcycles in 1923 and cars in 1928.

While motorcycles were a fairly simple proposition for engineers of BMW's caliber, automobiles proved more difficult. BMW tried to design its own automobile, but the economics of doing so led the company to shortcut the process by buying an existing automaker instead. It found one for sale in Thuringia, about 250 miles east of Munich, where the Eisenach Vehicle Factory built British-designed Austin Sevens under license and sold them under its Dixi nameplate.

Taking over the Eisenach factory at the end of 1928, BMW began applying its engineering acumen to improve the Dixi to race-winning form. With the Austin license's expiration pending in

1932, BMW needed an all-new automobile to stay in business.

That automobile became the 303. Introduced in 1933, the 303 possessed all of the ingredients that would define BMW's automobiles for the next 90 years.

First was the inline six-cylinder engine, the liquid-cooled M303 whose configuration had been insisted upon by managing director Franz Josef Popp, himself a mechanical engineer. The 1,182cc M303 effectively added two cylinders to BMW's first series-production automotive engine, the M68a four that debuted a year earlier. It borrowed the American technique of casting the crankcase and the cylinder block as a unit: The block was split at the centerline of the four-bearing crankshaft, its bottom half crafted in sheet metal.

The M303 was designed by Karl Rech and Rudolf Schleicher. Little can be learned about Rech at this point—in 1931, he succeeded the legendary Max Friz as BMW's technical director when Friz's aero and motorcycle engine expertise failed to translate into automobiles—but Schleicher remains a seminal figure in BMW history.

Born in Munich in 1897, Schleicher joined BMW in 1922, immediately upon earning his engineering degree at the city's technical university. Within a year, he was running BMW's motorcycle division. A cylinder head expert as well as a keen racing enthusiast, Schleicher led BMW to the racing victories that established its reputation for reliability and technical excellence. In 1927, Schleicher's experiments with supercharged motorcycle engines drew Friz's ire. When Friz ordered him to cease testing, Schleicher left BMW for rival automaker Horch. In Zwickau, he became Horch's head of research and development, reporting to Fritz Fiedler, the company's lead automotive engineer. Four years later, however, Schleicher was persuaded by motorcycle racer Ernst Henne to return to BMW.

The 1933-'34 303, BMW's first all-new car of its own design.

Fiedler was born in Potsdam, near Berlin, in 1899. He'd worked for Stöwer in Stettin before joining Horch, and he wasn't happy when Horch became part of Auto Union in 1932. When Schleicher invited him to BMW that year, Fiedler accepted.

His aptitude was recognized immediately. Though Alfred Böning had been in charge of BMW's automobile section while the company was revising the Austin Seven, responsibility for the overall design of BMW's first all-new car was assigned to Fiedler instead.

Crucially, Fiedler designed its chassis under the principle of *Leichtbau*, or "lightweight construction," which endowed the 303 and all of the BMWs that followed with exceptional handling. *Leichtbau* went against the automotive industry's prevailing wisdom, which held that a heavier car would have better roadholding than a lighter one. Fiedler believed otherwise, and he designed the 303 with a stiff-but-light tubular A-shaped frame, compliant suspension that benefited from low unsprung weight, and strong brakes to match its 30-hp engine.

The 303 evolved rapidly into the 315 and 319, the model designations reflecting increasing engine displacements of 1,490 and 1,911cc and outputs of 34 and 45 horsepower, respectively. In 1934, BMW introduced the 315/1 and 319/1, genuine sporting roadsters that gave BMW its first taste of circuit-racing success on tracks like the Nürburgring.

The 303 line reached its apotheosis with the 328, a purebred sports car that made its public debut at the 1936 Nürburgring *Eifelrennen*. Racing in the 2.0-liter sports car race—a support class to the German Grand Prix for purpose-built race cars—the 328 created the sensation of the weekend when motorcycle speed record ace Ernst Henne raced it to victory in front of some 250,000 spectators. Driving a pre-production 328 prototype, Henne averaged

An evolution of the 303, the 1937-'40 328 became the dominant sports racer of its time.

63.5 mph over five laps and nearly 70 miles to beat his nearest competitor (in a supercharged Alfa) by two minutes, 27 seconds.

Though Henne would soon retire from racing, his victory was only the beginning of the 328's remarkable run. Schleicher had designed the M328 engine with a hemispherical combustion chamber and an ingenious valvetrain that allowed the triple-carburetor 1,971cc six to put out 80 hp at a then-astronomical 5,000 rpm. With strong Lockheed hydraulic brakes, and superb handling thanks to front transverse leaf spring and rear semi-elliptic spring suspension, the 1,830-lb. roadster became the sports car of choice for gentleman racers in the 2.0-liter class, particularly in Germany and Great Britain. A handful of 328s came to the US, too, one of which won the 1939 Mt. Washington hillclimb with John Ewell at the wheel.

While scoring countless wins for privateers, the 328 was also a formidable weapon for BMW's factory team, which modified the M328 engine to put out as much as 130 hp. Aided by an aerodynamic coupe body by Touring of Milan, the 328 earned BMW a class victory in the 1939 24 Hours of Le Mans, and the overall win at the 1940 *Gran Premio Brescia delle Mille Miglia*.

Though BMW moved on to build larger, more luxurious models like the 326 and 335, designed for comfortable high-speed cruising on Germany's new *autobahns*, the 328 remained the heart and soul of its automotive division. It also defined BMW in the public imagination, giving the marque an indelible association with lightweight construction, agile handling, and reliable, race-winning performance in an everyday-usable package.

Throughout the 1920s and '30s, BMW's motorcycles and cars won races and sold strongly, but neither generated much profit compared to BMW's aero engines.

BMW's Factory Number 1 in Munich's Milbertshofen neighborhood had begun building aero engines again when the Treaty of Versailles' restrictions were lifted in 1923. Its nine-cylinder 132 radial (a refinement of a Pratt & Whitney design) powered aircraft like the Junkers Ju 52 used by Swissair and Lufthansa as well as the German air force.

BMW's military contracts became increasingly important once again after 1933, when Adolf Hitler took power and began re-arming Germany for war. From 1932 to 1939, BMW's workforce expanded from 3,000 to 27,000 employees, most of whom were building aero engines for the military.

Eventually, the Luftwaffe's appetite for aero engines could no longer be satisfied by what could be produced by BMW in Munich-Milbertshofen. In 1939, BMW built a far larger plant in Allach, about six miles northwest

(Left) Junkers Ju 52 with BMW 132 radials. (Right) Messerschmitt Me262 with BMW 003 jet engines.

of BMW's home plant, but soon even that wasn't enough. In 1940, following the invasion of Poland and other acts of aggression that ignited the Second World War, the Nazi government ordered BMW to dedicate all of Milbertshofen's capacity to aero engines. Motorcycle production (by then exclusively for the military) was sent to Eisenach, and civilian automobile production in that plant ceased altogether.

Focusing almost completely on aero engines, BMW was on the cutting edge of developments for engine control systems, direct fuel injection, and other technologies. Again, BMW engines became the preferred powerplants of Luftwaffe pilots, just as they'd been during the first global conflict.

By 1944, BMW's Milbertshofen and Allach plants were churning out thousands upon thousands of piston-powered radial engines, built in part by forced laborers from the Dachau concentration camp just up the road. At the same time, BMW's engineers were designing and building some of the world's first jet engines, as well as rockets.

The Allies were well aware of BMW's importance to the Nazi war machine, and BMW's factories became a prime target of Allied bombing raids. By the time World War II ended in Germany's defeat, the Milbertshofen plant had been almost completely destroyed, and what little remained would be dismantled by the occupying US Army after 1945. About 40% of BMW's factory in Eisenach was still operational at war's end, but that plant fell within the Soviet zone of occupation; by 1952, it would be lost to BMW forever.

The massive Allach engine plant, on the other hand, came through the bombing nearly undamaged thanks to its effective camouflage and somewhat remote location in the woods north of Munich. At war's end, it was seized by the US Army and renamed the Karlsfeld Ordnance Depot. Performing maintenance and repair of military vehicles, Karlsfeld kept BMW in business, and the revenue it generated allowed BMW to rebuild its plant in Munich-Milbertshofen.

At first, the factory produced only everyday necessities like pots and pans; eventually, bicycles were added. In 1948, the occupying authorities permitted BMW to produce small motorcycles, and in 1952 they allowed the plant to build its first automobiles.

Germany's economy had yet to fully recover from the destruction wrought by war, however, and neither had BMW.

The country needed an inexpensive small car to get moving again, and that's what chief engineer Alfred Böning wanted to build. Instead, he was directed by sales manager

The 1952-'58 501 "Baroque Angel" and lead engineer Alfred Böning.

Hanns Grewenig to create a luxury sedan, since BMW wasn't yet capable of producing any vehicle in the volumes required to make a small car profitable. Grewenig also put the brakes on a low-volume sports car like the 328. Even though racing had begun again in Germany, he decreed that building a high-end, high-profit margin sedan was the only way to put the company back on its feet.

Böning complied, and his 501 and 502 sedans constituted a technical tour de force. Unfortunately, they were cloaked in outdated bodywork (by Peter Szymanowski, who'd been head of body production at the Eisenach plant from 1938 to '45) that earned them the nickname "Baroque Angels." Large and elegant, but relatively underpowered even when equipped with BMW's—and the world's —first light-alloy V8, the 501 and 502 were almost exactly what postwar Germans didn't need, and most certainly couldn't afford. The same could be said for the sportier 503 and 507 that came along a few years later, designed for the American market but doomed by high prices no matter where they were offered.

In 1956, BMW finally built a car suited to German market conditions. Licensing production of the Isetta microcar from Italy's Iso, BMW replaced its two-stroke engine with a 250cc four-stroke and reinforced its chassis for much better handling. The BMW-built Isetta sold like hotcakes to customers eager to move up from motorcycles.

It arrived just in time. Motorcycles had gotten Germany rolling again after the war, but sales tanked suddenly in the late '50s: From a high of 29,500 in 1954, BMW's annual motorcycle production fell to just 5,429 three years later. Isetta production filled the gap, boosting BMW's automobile output from 4,567 cars in 1955 to 35,483 in 1956. But although Isettas kept the line humming, they generated very little profit.

The 700 is shown to the BMW board at Starnberg in July 1958. Chairman Heinrich Richter-Brohm, planning director Helmut-Werner Bönsch, and sales manager Ernst Hof stand behind the car.

Moreover, BMW's product strategy meant it had nothing to offer customers between the Isetta and the Baroque Angels: no high-volume, midrange car that would appeal to the masses as Germany's economy improved. Left out of the *Wirtschaftswunder* (economic miracle), BMW was on the brink of bankruptcy by 1959, its major shareholders ready to sell the company to Daimler-Benz.

The company needed a savior, and it found two. The first was a small car called the 700, the second an investor named Herbert Quandt.

The 700 was a joint development between BMW in Munich and the company's Austrian importer, Wolfgang Denzel. Born in Vienna in 1908, Denzel's family owned a foundry, and he was educated as an engineer. An enthusiast of racing on two and four wheels as well as skis, Denzel built his own motorcycle during World War II. In 1948, he began converting Volkswagens into Denzel-badged sports cars, which he built until 1960.

As BMW's representative in Austria, Denzel met frequently in Vienna with BMW board chairman Dr. Heinrich Richter-Brohm. He had a vested interest in BMW's product strategy, and he advised Richter-Brohm to build a real small car as a bridge to the profitable midrange sector. Richter-Brohm commissioned Denzel to design just such a car, and in July 1958 Denzel presented the 700 to a group of BMW executives at Lake Starnberg.

Denzel's new car was based on the 600, introduced by BMW in 1957 as a larger and more powerful variation on the Isetta, with a longer wheelbase and seating for four. Denzel used the 600's opposed-twin motorcycle engine in the familiar location behind the rear axle, but he gave the car a wider footprint and stylish coupe bodywork designed by Giovanni Michelotti. Crucially, Michelotti located the 700's doors where customers wanted them: on either side of the passenger compartment rather than at the front, like an Isetta or 600.

The response at Starnberg was immediate if not unanimous. After overcoming obstruction by those executives who had no interest in a car that originated in Vienna rather than Munich, BMW approved the 700 for production, with considerable input from the engineers in Munich, particularly with respect to the car's unit-body construction, BMW's first.

The 700 coupe drew raves at a press preview in June 1959, and the kudos continued when it was shown alongside a Michelotti-designed sedan variant at the Frankfurt auto show that September. The positive response turned into tens of thousands of advance orders: 15,000 in Germany, 10,000 from the US.

Before the 700 could be built, however, BMW first had to weather the financial crisis engendered in large part by the decommissioning of the Karlsfeld Ordnance Depot in 1955. Without the revenues from its maintenance work for the US Army, BMW could no longer prop up low-volume car manufacturing.

BMW had resumed small-scale aircraft engine production at Allach, but it had little hope of regaining its wartime technical excellence. With its best engineers putting their talents to use elsewhere—fighting the Cold War between the Soviet Union and its former allies France, Great Britain, and the US—Germany's aviation industry had fallen far behind. In 1960, BMW decided to sell 50% of Allach to MAN.

Just before that was due to occur, the annual shareholders' meeting in December 1959 saw BMW's Board of Supervisors ready to sell the entire company to Daimler-Benz. Several of

those supervisors were heavily invested in Daimler, too, and they stood to gain smartly from turning BMW into a Daimler subsidiary.

Which they would have done had a few small shareholders not exercised their rights to examine BMW's books before they'd agree to release their shares. In doing so, they discovered that development costs for the 700 had been allocated to a single year rather than amortized across several, as is normal, and that the company had failed to calculate advance orders for the new car. With those two factors rectified, the situation looked much more promising for BMW.

Enter Herbert Quandt.

Then 49, Quandt was the second son of industrialist Gunther Quandt, who'd made a fortune supplying uniforms to the German military during World War I. After that war, Gunther purchased a battery manufacturer, a potash mine, and a metal fabricating business. When World War II came along, Gunther Quandt again profited handsomely from military contracts…and the use of slave labor. He created an industrial empire that was taken over by his sons, half-brothers Herbert and Harald, while Gunther was interned by the Allies from 1946 to '48.

Herbert had been almost blind from the age of nine, but he was keen to assume his role in the family business nonetheless after World War II ended. With Harald, he increased and diversified the Quandt empire considerably during the postwar period. By Gunther's death in 1954, the Quandts had controlling interests in some 200 companies, and Herbert was a major shareholder in both BMW and Daimler.

Though he stood to gain from the latter's acquisition of BMW, Quandt was convinced by the small shareholders' demonstration of loyalty not to sell but to increase his holdings

The New Class 1500 sedan on display at the Frankfurt auto show in September 1961.

in BMW. He ended up staking around half his personal fortune in the company, and his investment kept BMW independent.

It was by no means a sure thing. BMW had recorded a loss of DM 14.7 million ($3.52 million) in 1959, and it continued to lose money for another four years despite the infusion of Quandt capital and strong sales for the 700, which went into production in January 1960.

Fortunately for Quandt and BMW, the 700 was a tremendous hit. The car became known as the "workingman's Porsche" thanks not only to its rear-mounted engine but also to its agile handling and spirited performance in a compact package. Before long, racing grids were full of 700s just like they'd been full of 328s in the late 1930s.

The success of the 700 justified Quandt's investment, but even more important was the "New Class" sedan already in the pipeline by the time the crisis hit in 1959.

The New Class sedan was being engineered by BMW's best and brightest from the prewar period. These men were no longer young, but they brought a tradition of excellence to the task, and they were determined to produce a real BMW despite the severe budgetary constraints imposed by the company's tenuous finances.

First among them was project director Fritz Fiedler, who'd pioneered the 303's *Leichtbau* construction. Fiedler spent 1947 through 1950 working for BMW's prewar British importer, HJ Aldington, updating 328 principles to make new automobiles for Bristol and Frazer-Nash before returning to Germany. After a brief stint at Opel, Fiedler came "home" to BMW in 1952, working on the 503 and 507 before being put in charge of the New Class sedan's overall development in 1960. He was 61 years old, resuming the same position he'd held nearly three decades earlier, when he'd created his revolutionary BMWs with

Engineers Wilhelm Hofmeister, Fritz Fiedler, Eberhard Wolff, and Alex von Falkenhausen in 1970.

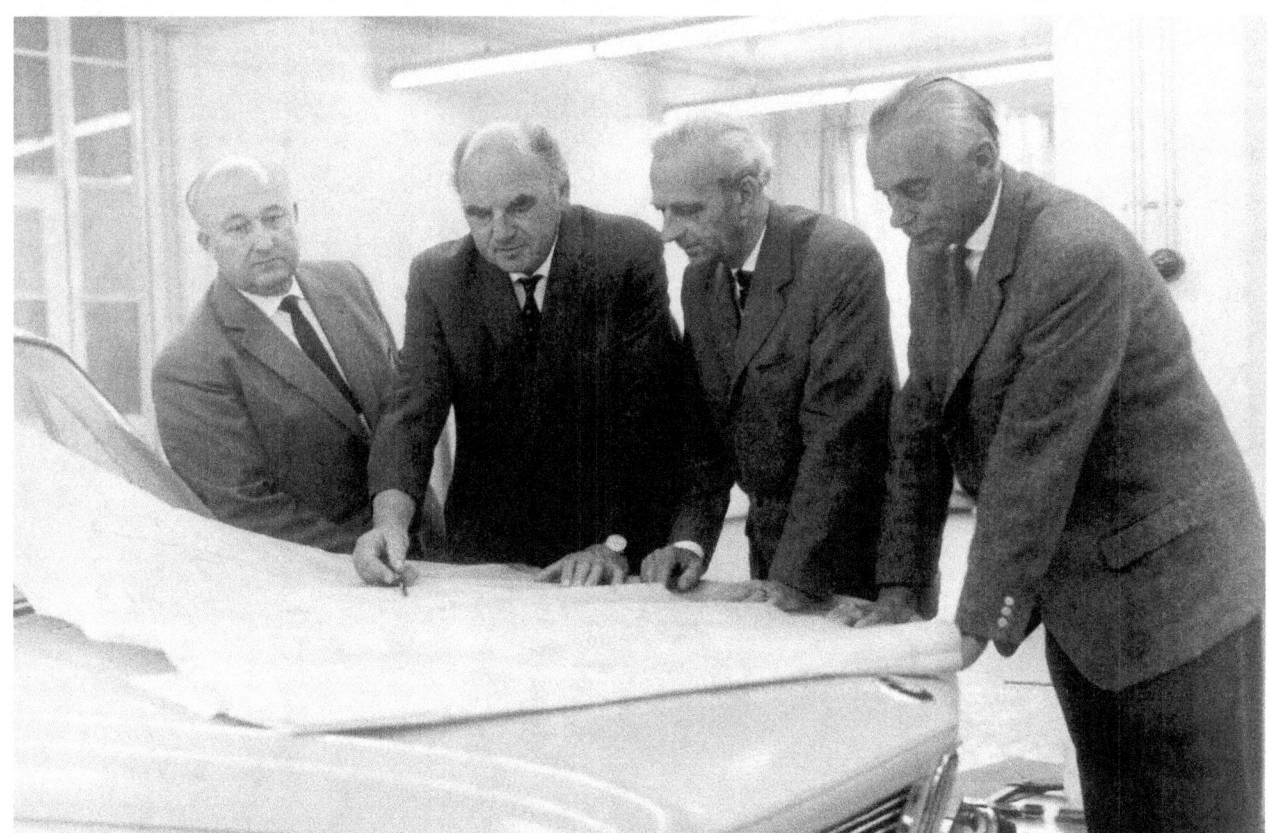

Rudolf Schleicher. (Schleicher never returned to BMW after the war, opting to run his own camshaft company instead.)

Second was Alexander von Falkenhausen, in charge of engine development. Then 53, he'd joined BMW's motorcycle division in 1934, fresh from Munich's technical university. An enthusiastic racer on two and four wheels, von Falkenhausen designed BMW's first rear suspension for motorcycles, used on its production bikes from 1938 to '56. He spent the war years developing the R75 military motorcycle, riding it almost to Stalingrad before turning back for Eisenach, having figured out how to keep dirt and debris from its suspension and engine.

In 1935, von Falkenhausen bought a factory-prepped 315/1 roadster, which he raced before trading it for a 328 in 1939. When World War II broke out, he hid his 328 in a barn for the duration, and as soon as the war was over he dug it out and went racing again. From 1948, von Falkenhausen built 328-based F2 racers and sports cars under his own AFM nameplate, but his operation was chronically underfunded, and he closed up shop in 1952. Returning to BMW in 1954, he was tasked with improving the 507's performance, and in 1957 he became head of BMW's engine department.

For the New Class sedan, von Falkenhausen designed an all-new four-cylinder engine. Like Schleicher in the early 1930s, he did so with Karl Rech, who continued to develop the

The New Class 1500 sedan in Munich, 1962.

modular engine concept that had been used to create the M303 six-cylinder from the M68a four. This time, however, economics dictated a four-cylinder. The resulting 1.5-liter M115 was a masterpiece of durability, with five main bearings supporting a counterbalanced and forged crankshaft. The block was cast iron, the cylinder head aluminum, with a single overhead camshaft driven by a double-row chain. Equipped with a single Solex carburetor, the engine put out 75 horsepower when the 1500 debuted at the Frankfurt auto show in 1961, and 80 hp at 5,700 rpm by the time it went into production in 1962.

[Note: In 1980, BMW rationalized its internal engine codes, re-naming the M115 and its descendants the M10. We'll use M10 throughout this book when referring to all four-cylinder engines of this design.]

The New Class' chassis was the province of Eberhard Wolff. Like von Falkenhausen, Wolff had worked in BMW's motorcycle division, where he was tasked with keeping the Munich machines competitive in Grand Prix racing after the FIM banned supercharging in 1946. By 1954, he was head of development for the car division. Wolff had spotted Iso's Isetta at the Geneva auto show, obtaining a license to build it at BMW and developing it into a much better car than the Italian original.

Wolff's unit-construction chassis for the New Class sedan had a wheelbase of 100.5 inches, with track widths of 52 inches front, 54 inches rear. Wolff had specified MacPherson strut front suspension that linked to control arms at the bottom, paired with the semi-trailing arm rear suspension first seen on the 600 microcar, with coil springs and hydraulic dampers. Rubber bushings isolated the suspension from the body, and a front anti-roll bar was standard along with 14-inch wheels, four-wheel drum brakes, and worm-and-roller steering.

In charge of New Class styling and body engineering was Wilhelm Hofmeister, who had succeeded Peter Szymanowski as head of BMW's styling department in 1955. Born in 1912, he was mechanical engineer, not a designer per se—even though his name is attached to the "Hofmeister kink" at the rear window of every BMW since the Bertone-designed 3200 CS of 1961.

For the New Class, Hofmeister supervised the work of Giovanni Michelotti, who'd been under contract with BMW since 1957. Commuting between Turin and Munich, Michelotti drafted a body that looked every bit as modern as the technology underpinning the new sedan.

The 1500 caused a sensation when it was shown at Frankfurt in 1961, and showgoers had to wait in long lines just to catch a glimpse of it. Despite some early quality-control problems, it became a tremendous hit upon reaching production. It looked nothing like the prewar 328 roadster, but the New Class shared that car's essential BMW virtues of light weight, superb handling, and just-right power.

The 1500 tipped the scales at 2,332 lbs., and it accelerated from zero to 62 mph in 16.0 seconds en route to a top speed of 92 mph—crisp performance in 1963, the first full year that the new 1500 was sold alongside the 700

That year, BMW turned a small profit: DM 3.8 million, or $952,381. BMW earned DM 6.5 million in 1964, and in 1965 profits increased to DM 9.2 million, boosted by BMW's sale of the rest of the Allach plant to MAN.

Having divested itself of the aircraft engine business at last, BMW would have to succeed on the strength of its cars and motorcycles alone, products that had been almost incidental to in its pre-1945 business plan. More crucially, BMW would have to export its cars and motorcycles profitably, particularly to the large and lucrative US market.

That it could do so was by no means guaranteed. The New Class was a certified hit in Germany, but it hadn't really caught on with US car buyers despite its technical excellence. From 1962 through '65, BMW exported just 2,167 New Class sedans to the US.

To crack the US market, BMW needed something sportier and more stylish, yet still practical and affordable. As it turned out, BMW had exactly such a car in the works, identified internally as the Type 114.

"Niche Paul" creates a new one

The crisis of 1959 had been provoked in large part by BMW's failed product strategy, and the company was overdue for a management shakeup when Herbert Quandt (**opposite, right**) acquired his majority stake in 1960. Almost immediately, Quandt began remaking the BMW board, bringing in trusted executives from other organizations within the Quandt Group and hiring others from rival automakers.

BMW's first postwar technical director Kurt Donath and sales chief Hanns Grewenig had resigned in 1957, replaced by Dr. Heinrich Richter-Brohm and Ernst Hof, respectively. Richter-Brohm stepped down in the wake of the shareholder's revolt of 1959, while sales chief Hof switched roles with purchasing manager Ernst Kämpfer. Kämpfer then served as both sales chief and acting general manager until October 1961, when Paul Hahnemann (**opposite, left**) arrived to take over sales and marketing.

By then, Quandt had also seated Wilhelm Gieschen on the BMW board as technical director. Gieschen came to BMW from Borgward, where he'd been chief engineer at the well-regarded but financially undercapitalized and poorly managed firm in Bremen. Gieschen wasn't alone in leaving Borgward for BMW: Karl Monz came to Munich as board member for purchasing, along with a number of talented engineers.

Quandt hired Hahnemann from Auto Union, where he'd been marketing director since 1957. Born in Strasbourg in 1912, Hahnemann had earned degrees in business management and engineering before starting his career with General Motors in Detroit. He returned to Germany in 1939 to work at Adam Opel AG, a GM subsidiary since 1929.

Like most automobile manufacturers, Opel converted its production facilities to produce military goods during World War II, in this case tanks and airplane parts. (Ironically, that put General Motors in the position of profiting from military production on both sides of the conflict.) At war's end, Hahnemann was labeled by the Allies as "indispensable" to the German military-industrial complex, and he was detained by the French for 37 months. Hahnemann returned to Opel after his release in 1948, but in 1957 he left the GM subsidiary to become marketing director of Auto Union.

Hahnemann had broad experience, and a deep understanding of the automobile business. He was nicknamed "Niche Paul" for his ability to commission products that would fill every possible market segment, allowing a brand to retain customers as they moved up the ladder to larger, more sophisticated models.

His talents were well known throughout the industry, and Auto Union's late '50s instability—it was acquired by Daimler in 1958—made Hahnemann a target for other carmakers, including BMW.

His personal style was flamboyant and somewhat abrasive, however, and it didn't really fit with BMW's sober, engineering-oriented culture. Not everyone within the company was on board with his arrival, and their trepidation saw Hahnemann named to the board first as a deputy rather than a full member.

He arrived in Munich on September 1, 1961, a few weeks before the 1500 debuted at the Frankfurt auto show. The new sedan wasn't ready for production, but its pending arrival had caused sales of the still-available 700 to slump badly in anticipation.

Hahnemann's first tour of the Milbertshofen factory revealed thousands of unsold 700s even as more were rolling off the line. Told domestic dealers were overstocked, Hahnemann started calling BMW's European importers, threatening to terminate their contracts if they didn't accept more cars. By the end of the day, he'd moved nearly all unsold inventory and banked DM 6 million in sales.

As BMW executive Oscar Kolk told historian Horst Mönnich, "That was his opening act, and it opened up the doors—upwards, to as far as Quandt, to whom Hahnemann's style had such little appeal." It also had the effect, Kolk said, of energizing BMW from top to bottom, at

Georg Bertram's sketch of March 4, 1960, suggesting a 1,000cc version of the 700.

headquarters and at the dealerships.

Hahnemann brought more to BMW than his skills of persuasion. Having come up through the ranks at GM subsidiary Opel, Hahnemann knew what made a "real" car company: not just sales but service, spare parts, and, most importantly, marketing.

Hahnemann conducted some of BMW's first real market research, and it revealed what the shareholders of 1959 had already known: that BMW had one of the strongest brands in the automotive industry. In public perception, the essence of BMW lay not in postwar cars like the Baroque Angels or the Isetta but in the 328 and 327: the sporty, agile machines that made BMW's reputation in the 1930s.

That spirit carried on in the 700 Sport, but BMW had nothing to offer customers keen to move on to larger automobiles but without the necessary cash to jump from a 700 Sport priced at DM 5,850 ($1,463) to a 1500 sedan at DM 9,485 ($2,371).

The gap between a 1500 sedan and 1961's least-expensive Baroque Angel at DM 15,450 ($3,863) was of less concern than the absence of a small car between the 700 and the 1500. Hahnemann knew the microcar's days were numbered, and he also knew that BMW risked losing customers to other marques if it failed to build a small car to fit into the niche above the existing 700 but below the forthcoming 1500.

Fortunately, the 700's replacement was already being contemplated by the time Hahnemann arrived at BMW.

As design drawings reveal, BMW had been working on the 700's successor since 1960. The company had commissioned Giovanni Michelotti to draft a new small two-door, and Georg Bertram was doing so in-house at BMW.

Bertram's sketches are in the BMW Design Archive in Garching, near Munich, and they provide a fascinating window into the process by which BMW created its new small car.

On March 4, 1960, Bertram sketched a sporty-looking two-door identified as a "BMW 1000," which looks like a more powerful and slightly more substantial variant of the existing 700.

Two days later, Bertram drew an entirely different two-door: a somewhat Corvair-like

Bertram's sketch of March 6, 1960, showing a thoroughly redesigned—and larger—BMW coupe.

two-door with a real coupe roofline and a character line delineated with a chrome strip. Its taillights are borrowed from the 700, but otherwise the car appears all-new.

On May 2, Bertram completed another plan view of his car from March 4. On this drawing, he specifies a 98-inch wheelbase, 161.4-inch overall length and a 55-inch height. Notes on the drawing car identify the car as a BMW 1200 2-Door Limousine, to be built by a partner coachworks with an engine from 1,200 to 1,600cc.

Bertram's efforts in the design studio would seem to have been commissioned from the executive suite, although research by Manfred Grunert at the BMW Archive identifies February 1962—two years later—as the start of deliberations on a new car to slot in below the New Class sedan.

Given the management shakeup happening on the board throughout 1960 and 1961, as well as the company's focus on developing the 1500, it makes sense that the smaller car would remain in the background prior to 1962. Once the 1500 had been launched successfully, however, BMW's executives could turn their attention to the other "niches" in the product lineup.

At the Board of Management meeting in February 1962, newly-arrived chairman Dr. Karl-Heinz Sonne (appointed by Herbert Quandt to head BMW after seven years at the helm of the Quandt Group's Concordia Elektrizität AG) encouraged the creation of a "genuine BMW," powered by a 1.3–1.5-liter engine.

In keeping with BMW's successful collaborations with Michelotti, Bertone, and other Italians, Sonne wanted the car to be designed and constructed by an Italian coachbuilder. It would be ready in three to four years, preceded by a more powerful version of the 700—perhaps the one sketched by Bertram in 1960—that would remain in the lineup below the new car.

Hahnemann advocated for such a vehicle, too, defining it further as a "lower midrange car" that would be smaller and less expensive than the New Class sedan.

Examining records in the BMW Archive reveals a tortured gestation for BMW's new small car. The company was cash-poor despite Quandt's investment, and it had to rely on profits from the 1500 to fund new projects.

As a consequence, the car proposed by Sonne and Hahnemann wasn't assigned its own development code, Type 114, until late 1963.

Schematics of the M115 (later M10) four-cylinder engine and the Type 114 chassis.

Even then, the board continued to debate its character. Hahnemann—who'd been named full member of the board that April—wanted to make the Type 114 "a car with something special, using the 1500 engine, a lively car." He described a two-door whose model range could later include an estate car or wagon.

BMW was still contemplating a replacement for the 700 in addition to this new small car just above it, but Hahnemann now argued that a 700-like automobile had "no future." The market for such small cars was disappearing, and in any case BMW lacked the production capacity to build three cars—the 700's successor, the Type 114, and the New Class sedan—at Milbertshofen. (BMW's V8-powered 3200 CS of 1962–'65 was designed and built by Bertone in Turin, Italy.)

Throughout 1964, Hahnemann and Sonne continued to argue that the 700 line should be jettisoned in favor of the Type 114 and the New Class. They also continued to advocate for the Type 114 as a two-door powered by the sedan's 1.5-liter four-cylinder engine.

The discussions show that both Hahnemann and Sonne understood the essence of BMW. They were determined to make sure that the company's next small car would be a "real BMW" in the eyes of those who remembered the 328, or who'd enjoyed their 700s in races and rallies. They advocated for frisky performance in a compact package, a car that would be fun to drive despite being relatively simple and inexpensive.

BMW targeted a production date of September 1965 along with a price of DM 6,500 ($1,625). The board's indecision delayed production by four months, while engineering progress saw the car become slightly larger, heavier, and better built.

It used a unique body shell, one with a shorter wheelbase than the New Class sedan's: 98.4 inches rather than 100.4. That was slightly longer than the wheelbase proposed for the 700's upgraded successor but still short enough to give the Type 114 more agile handling than the New Class even as it borrowed the sedan's steering, suspension, and drivetrain parts.

Despite the economy of shared components, a new cost accounting pegged the Type 114's price at DM 8,250 ($2,063). The car was getting expensive, but Hahnemann felt the increase could be justified if the Type 114 were equipped with the slightly larger 1.6-liter M10 engine with 83 horsepower. That would give it an edge on the competition, and it would also provide a

Bertram's final sketch for the Type 114 exterior, executed May 4, 1965.

link to Formula 2, which was slated to switch from 1.0- to 1.6-liter engines in 1967. (BMW was developing its own F2 engines based on the production M10, which von Falkenhausen's robust construction had rendered capable of impressive power gains with no loss of reliability.)

While BMW's engineers were refining the car's specification, Bertram was perfecting its design. His final sketch of May 4, 1965 shows a diminished Corvair influence, though the chrome strip remains from his drawing of May 4, 1960, along with the peaks that define the outer edges of the hood and trunk lid. The car now has round headlights and taillights. Bertram's "combination taillight," penned on October 28, 1964, borrowed its round shape from the taillights on the Giorgetto Giugiaro-designed 3200 CS, adding chrome elements and an amber turn signal lens.

Bertram's final design shows the influence, too, of the four-cylinder 2000 C/CS designed in-house at BMW. The Type 114 borrows its shark-like profile from the 2000 coupe, along with its sleeker sides and single character line.

Even as he followed the basic template established by the New Class sedan, Bertram designed the Type 114 to emphasize its youthful, sporty nature without diminishing its apparent practicality. It's less boxy than the sedan, with edges rounded off to diminish its overall dimensions and a less upright greenhouse whose pillars taper inward gracefully. As with all good designs, it improves under close scrutiny, revealing a wealth of details to fascinate the eye: the textured surfaces on some trim pieces, the chrome gas cap, the neatly-integrated turn signals. It's a masterpiece of mid-'60s design, and it undoubtedly played a role in the car's enduring success.

The Type 114 was for all purposes finished by late spring 1965, but its fate was debated yet again on September 15 that year. This time, the Supervisory Board was questioning the car's viability, since it wouldn't be profitable until BMW had sold 100,000 units. An organization of shareholders and executives above the Board of Management, the Supervisory Board had ultimate authority over expenditures, and its members agreed to build the Type 114 only after strenuous arguments from Hahnemann and technical director Wilhelm Gieschen.

One month later, the car got a name: 1600. To avoid confusion with the sedan, the New Class 1600 would henceforth be called the 1600 V, for

1600 production at Milbertshofen in 1966. While parts of the line were automated, much of the component assembly and finish work was completed by hand.

Vier (four) doors. That proved cumbersome and confusing, and soon the four-door was again the 1600 while the two-door became the 1600-2. Both were badged as 1600s, however, and a 1967 price list identifies them as the "1600 Sedan 2 Door" and "1600 Sedan 4 Door." Their owners referred to them simply as 1600s, or as 1602s after the name change of April 1971.

Production of the 1600-2 began in March 1966, with 150 cars per day emerging from Milbertshofen. 1600-2s thus constituted about one-third of Milbertshofen's total output. The rest—about 300 cars per day—was given over to the New Class and 700, while the 2000 CS was built by Karmann in Osnabrück.

The 1600-2 slots in

BMW had planned to debut the 1600-2 at the Geneva auto show, but a last-minute change of plans saw the car make its first public appearance in front of the Munich opera house, where BMW was holding its 50th anniversary celebration on March 9, 1966. Set among a 328 roadster and Ernst Henne's speed record bike, the 1600-2 sent an unmistakable signal: BMW was building real sports cars again.

A day later, the 1600-2 had its planned introduction at the Geneva auto show, part of BMW's thoroughly revamped lineup. Gone were the Baroque Angels and Isettas; now, the show stand was filled by modern two- and four-door sedans, plus the stylish 2000 CS coupe.

Like the New Class 1500 sedan in 1961, the 1600-2 was a hit from the start. Even though its DM 8,650 ($2,163) base price was higher than planned, the car was still affordable, especially since the performance of the 1.6-liter engine had improved from 83 to 85 DIN horsepower with the fitting of a larger Solex 38 PDSI carburetor in place of the Solex 36-40 PDSI used in the New Class 1600. (That car left the lineup as the two-door 1600-2 went into production, which eliminated some confusion regarding BMW's pair of similarly-named automobiles.)

The 1600-2's instant popularity saw the Milbertshofen plant running full tilt by August, straining to keep up with demand. A shortage of both space and skilled labor restricted production to about 450 cars per day, though the market could have absorbed 600.

The situation prompted BMW to do the same thing it had done when it became an automaker in 1928: buy an existing carmaker. This time, the target was Hans Glas GmbH, a maker of agricultural machinery that had scored big in the 1950s with its Goggo scooter and Goggomobil microcar. Based in Dingolfing, about 60 miles northeast of Munich, Glas also produced a stylish hatchback and a V8-powered sedan, both with bodywork by Pietro Frua.

Regardless of size, Glas vehicles were known for their technical excellence and innovation, like the belt-driven camshaft that former BMW engineer Leonhard Ischinger had patented at Glas. Those developments required a sizable budget, as did the essentially hand-built nature of Glas' full-size cars, which were produced in low volumes and generated small profits. The Glas family was debt-averse in the extreme, and by the mid-'60s the company was on the brink.

BMW's Grand Prix motorcycle ace Schorsch Meier sold both Glas and BMW products from his Munich dealership, and he put Andreas Glas in touch with Paul Hahnemann. Hahnemann recognized the opportunity to add both physical property and skilled workers by acquiring Glas, and he went to Herbert Quandt directly with the proposition. Quandt agreed, and soon BMW was taking over a rival Bavarian carmaker, with help from the Bavarian state bank.

The Glas factory itself was outdated and would need to be torn down before BMW could begin building its own cars there, but its 3,000 employees were capable of producing BMWs immediately, and most could commute to Milbertshofen to do so.

By 1968, the infusion of labor allowed production at BMW's home plant to increase to 500 cars daily. Even so, the wait list for a new 1600-2 stretched to eight months, which must have been hard for eager enthusiasts to bear.

By the standards of 1966, the 2,028-lb. 1600-2 offered exciting performance. With 8.6:1 compression and that single Solex carburetor, the 1,573cc M10 engine delivered 85 DIN horsepower at 5,700 rpm and 93 lb-ft at 3,000 rpm. The 1600-2 needed just 13.3 seconds to reach 62 mph on its way to a top speed of 99.4 mph. By comparison, the larger, heavier (by 326 lbs.), and slightly less powerful 1600 sedan need a full 14 seconds to hit 62 mph, and its top speed was 96.3 mph.

The 1600-2 was not only quicker, it was likely safer, too. It had strong brakes and four-wheel independent suspension, allowing its driver to avoid accidents actively. When that wasn't possible, it was strong enough to limit their severity. The 1600-2 was the first car that BMW

Crash-testing the 1600-2 in 1966. The crumple zones have absorbed the impact with the sedan.

crash-tested, using the rather primitive method of driving a New Class sedan into it. Photos of the result show a 1600-2 whose crumple zones have indeed crumpled, absorbing the energy of the impact while leaving its passenger compartment intact. The 1600-2 was equipped with a collapsible steering column, too, further reducing risk to the driver.

The 1600-2 certainly had an impact on BMW's annual production, which had already increased from 52,943 cars in 1961 to 67,709 in 1965 on demand for the New Class. With the arrival of the 1600-2, production increased to 74,076 cars in 1966, and to 87,618 in 1967 following the absorption of the Glas workforce.

Production capacity at the Munich plant remained severely constrained, however. As a result, BMW was primarily supplying the domestic market in Germany even as it estimated that exports would account for 35-40% of total Type 114 production in 1966.

BMW was especially eager to make a dent in the American market, which had been the world's largest since the end of World War II. In 1965, BMW had exported just 1,230 BMWs to the US, virtually all New Class sedans, and US importer Max Hoffman didn't see much potential in a two-door he regarded as a New Class derivative.

Specifically, Hoffman didn't think the 1600-2's four-cylinder engine—SAE rated at 96 horsepower, gross—would allow it to compete with sporty domestics like the Chevy Camaro or Ford Mustang. With six-cylinder engines, those cars delivered 140 and 115 hp, yet they were no more expensive than the 1600-2, priced at $2,477 in 1967.

The American cars may have had a horsepower advantage, but the 1600-2 had handling in its favor. Popular British imports like the Triumph TR4A and MGB roadster were its equal in handling, but the BMW was far more reliable. Over both the domestic and British competition, the BMW represented a vast improvement in build quality.

BMW's new two-door made a strong impression in its US debut at the New York auto show in April 1966, thanks in part to a publicity stunt that saw a 225-lb. lion make a *literal* impression on "Miss BMW," model Nell Theobald.

The lion—named Ludwig—had been brought to the show by the Grey PR firm to represent Bavaria at Hoffman's display. At first, Ludwig posed contentedly with Theobald, but he became annoyed by his handler in his second appearance and bit into Theobald's thigh. (Following a trip to the hospital, Theobald sued Hoffman, Grey, the NY Coliseum, and the show organizers for $3 million; in 1971, *The New York Times* reported, she settled for $250,000.)

Though Ludwig didn't perform quite as planned, the lion drew plenty of attention to the new BMW that served as the backdrop for his antics.

More important, the 1600-2 drew glowing reviews from the American automotive press. *Car and Driver* praised its performance and practicality, calling it the best $2,500 sedan the magazine had ever tested. *Road & Track* agreed. "It isn't as rich in details as the costlier

Cold-weather testing consisted of placing the entire 1600-2 in a freezer.

BMWs, but the materials are of good quality, in good taste, and put together well."

Road & Track rated the car's performance just as highly. "There is some body lean, but it isn't unsettling. The steering takes the car where it is pointed and with good bite at both ends."

The magazine reports were bolstered by clever advertising created for Hoffman by the James Neal Harvey agency in New York. The Harvey agency was young, founded in 1965, and it brought zest and irreverence to BMW's advertising. Principal Harvey had struck out on his own in New York after working for Young & Rubicam in Los Angeles, where he'd spent his spare time writing screenplays for television shows including *Dragnet*. His storytelling talent was on full display in the ads for BMW, which featured witty copy replete with technical detail and emotional appeal.

The ads touted the 1600-2's credentials as a sport sedan by virtue of its heritage, performance, and build quality. They were insouciant, almost taunting drivers to abandon lesser marques for the sophisticated pleasures of a BMW. The ads did a superb job of establishing the cars' slightly offbeat character, which could be truly understood only by the cognoscenti. A BMW wasn't for everyone; instead it was pitched toward car buyers who'd appreciate the stirring performance belied by its compact dimensions and restrained styling.

It's hard to believe in today's risk-averse climate, but the ads emphasized the car's ability to cruise comfortably at more than 100 mph. "That's right, this new BMW does 105 mph, is practically indestructible, and costs only $2,477. So what are you waiting for?" one ad asked.

"In Germany they say Be Em Vey. And they get out of the way," read one headline. "Move over" demanded another, showing a BMW in the rear-view window.

The ads weren't widely placed, but they were effective. To Hoffman's apparent surprise, the 1600-2 became a hit. Following the NY auto show, cars began trickling into the US even before a US-spec model went into production in August 1967; those early cars used a 6-volt electrical system, and they lacked the headrests, glare-free dash trim, padded steering wheel, and side reflectors required by the National Traffic and Motor Vehicle Safety Act of 1966.

By the end of 1967, BMW had exported 4,362 examples of the 1600-2 to the US. Total exports to the US climbed to 4,564 cars, a threefold increase over 1966's total.

If that was impressive, it was nothing compared to what was about to follow. The 1600-2 was about to get a new stablemate, one that would rewrite the book for BMW.

Hoffman Motors Corporation commissioned clever advertising from the James Neal Harvey agency upon the 1600-2's US debut in 1967.

In Germany they say Bey Em Vey. And they get out of the way.

How to get ahead.

2002: A Development History 35

The Max factor

That car, of course, was the 2002. It became BMW's most successful model to date almost from the moment it was introduced, a bona fide sensation worldwide. It became especially popular in the US, where its just-right combination of power and handling brought BMW to a much wider audience than the 1600-2 could ever reach.

Following the 2002's arrival, BMW's annual US exports doubled, reaching 9,172 cars by the end of 1968. With that kind of success, it was only natural that BMW's US importer at the time, Max Hoffman (**opposite**), would take credit for the 2002's inspiration, and his assertion continues to be repeated even today.

It's a dubious claim, but before we refute it, let's find out who Max Hoffman was, and examine his relationship to BMW's worldwide organization. Hoffman's importance to the BMW story predates the 2002, and it extends beyond the creation of a single BMW model.

First, it's important to note that foreign cars are really a postwar phenomenon, although a few came to the US earlier, like the Mercedes imported by Mitropa in the 1930s. Second, initial US imports were undertaken not by the British and European manufacturers but by independent businessmen who'd agreed to sell the cars in this country. Hoffman was one of the earliest to do so after World War II, and he was also one of the most prolific, representing a variety of marques starting in 1946. The name of his Hoffman Motors Corporation became well recognized thanks to its presence on advertisements for cars from Jaguar, Mercedes, Porsche, etc.

In 1972, Hoffman's role in introducing Americans to these cars was recognized in a mini-biography published in *Automobile Quarterly* in 1972. Entitled "The Baron of Park Avenue," for the location of Hoffman's New York City dealerships, the story was written by longtime automotive executive and journalist/historian Karl Ludvigsen.

At the time, Ludvigsen had no reason to suspect that the importer's relationship with BMW was about to change, or that Hoffman's version of events was slanted wildly in his own favor.

By April 1998, when Ludvigsen contributed a BMW-oriented version to the premiere issue of *Bimmer, the magazine about BMW*, he was able to revise the story significantly. Entitled "Motor Man Max," the later story included a brief but largely accurate account of Hoffman's termination as BMW's importer.

Unfortunately, *Bimmer* was a brand-new magazine and reached few readers in 1998, and the magazine never reproduced the story online. Most subsequent accounts, therefore, have relied on the far more flattering "Baron of Park Avenue," written while Hoffman was still BMW's US importer.

Even in 1998, however, Ludvigsen didn't have access to the full story. Nearly 20 years later, former BMW board member for sales Bob Lutz was interviewed for *Bimmer* by Marty Bernstein regarding the origins of the legendary "Ultimate Driving Machine" ad tagline. In describing the creation of BMW of North America, Lutz made some rather colorful comments about Hoffman, which inspired a follow-up query during another interview with Lutz in 2015, this one conducted by Bill Cobb.

As *Bimmer*'s editor, I wanted to dig deeper into the Hoffman matter, and in January 2017, I visited the BMW Archive and was granted access to board minutes and other relevant files from the era. Examining legal documents as well as notes from those who were involved in the process of BMW's extrication from its relationship with Hoffman, I discovered a situation that was far less straightforward than had ever been portrayed.

Max Hoffman may have introduced Americans to imported sports cars, but "The Baron of Park Avenue" is far less deserving of sports-car sainthood than that 1972 *Automobile Quarterly* article would have us believe.

Hoffman remains an intriguing figure, and a brief biography is warranted. Mark Edwin Hoffmann (his full legal name) was born in

A BMW 507 whose driver is identified by the BMW Archive as possibly Max Hoffman.

1904 near Vienna, Austria, where his father had inherited a general store that he turned into a manufacturer of sewing machines, then bicycles. The elder Hoffmann had one of the first automobiles in the area, and young Mark got a clip-on DKW engine for his bicycle in 1920. He began racing almost immediately, and by age 17 he'd graduated to a British-built AJS 350, with which he began winning.

Hoffmann's attention turned to four wheels when his father bought him a French-built Amilcar, which he raced until 1934. Deeming himself too old for racing, Hoffmann went into business, importing a variety of American, British, Italian, and French automobiles to Austria and representing European marques to the Middle East. All went well until Nazi Germany's *Anschluss* with Austria in 1938. Hoffmann's father was Jewish, and he could see the writing on the wall. He fled to the safety of Paris, only to watch the Nazis march into the French capital two years later, in the summer of 1940.

In 1941, Hoffmann emigrated to the US, planning to export trucks to Egypt upon his arrival. When that fell through, Hoffmann saw another opportunity in the wartime rationing of metal and the economic empowerment of women. He borrowed $300 to make metalized plastic jewelry, which he designed and produced, and in one week took $5,000 in orders.

The money he made from the jewelry business allowed Hoffmann to re-enter the automotive world in 1946, when he opened his automobile showroom at 487 Park Avenue with a single Delahaye on the floor.

By then, he'd begun calling himself Maximilian and had Americanized the spelling of his last name. As Ludvigsen wrote in *Automobile Quarterly*, "For his new venture in America he eliminated the last "n" from his surname and adopted, occasionally, the given name Maximilian as being more fitting, in New York, for a purveyor of exotic motorcars. He's proud of the name Max in its European frame of reference, yet recognizes that it carries little charisma when it's pronounced in American-accented English."

By 1948, Hoffman was Jaguar's official US importer. Other marques followed: Volkswagen, Porsche, Mercedes, Alfa, Lancia, Fiat…all told, Hoffman imported some 21 foreign marques to the US, most of which were coming to this country for the first time.

To help those marques succeed, Hoffman encouraged the creation of cars targeted specifically at the American market: the Mercedes 300SL and 190SL, the Porsche Speedster, the Alfa-Romeo Giulietta Spyder…

It wasn't all smooth sailing, however. Hoffman said he "gave up" on Volkswagen in 1953, unable to sell the cars. A 2005 story in *Automotive News* contradicts his assertion, reporting that "VW headquarters—recognizing the need for better organization and uniform standards in the growing U.S. market—canceled Hoffman's contract in 1953. The factory wanted the U.S. to reflect the 'service first and sales second' standard VW was using throughout the world."

That wasn't exactly Hoffman's motto, as we'll see later. In the meantime, he lost the Jaguar franchise in 1954, when William Lyons reportedly objected to Hoffman's growing involvement with Mercedes, which he'd begun importing in 1951, and his insistence that dealers accept Volkswagens in order to get Jaguars.

To get out of its contract, Jaguar was forced to pay Hoffman a substantial sum as well as a commission on every Jaguar sold in the US for years afterwards. Even in defeat, Hoffman drove a hard bargain.

After losing his lucrative Jaguar franchise as well as Volkswagen, Hoffman went to Munich to investigate the possibility of importing a high-volume BMW sports car to the US.

Hoffman had visited BMW on an earlier trip to Europe, but the company wasn't yet building cars in Munich. By 1954, production of the 501 and 502 was well underway, and other models were in the works. Of particular interest to Hoffman was a V8-powered two-seat sports car, his favorite body style. ("Every company he distributed, the first thing he set about doing was to create a two-seat sports car," said Lutz.)

Hoffman didn't like BMW's 528 roadster as designed by Ernst Loof, deeming it so ugly as to be unsaleable. For a redesign, he put BMW in touch with German-born American designer Albrecht von Goertz, who modeled what became the 507. (In a 1980 interview with *Porsche Panorama* magazine, Hoffman told Betty Jo Turner that he'd directed Goertz' efforts, which the designer would probably dispute were either man still alive.)

While the resulting car was undoubtedly beautiful, far more so than the prototype seen by Hoffman in 1954, it also helped drive BMW to near-bankruptcy when its development became much more expensive than planned.

First, Goertz' design required costly changes to the car's chassis before the car could be shown at Frankfurt in 1955. Second, Hoffman overestimated and/or misled BMW with regard to US demand for such a car. Finally, he failed to fulfill his agreed-upon commitments with respect to orders and payments.

Hoffman knew the US market was price-sensitive, which is why he'd encouraged Porsche to build the minimally-equipped Speedster from the 356 Cabriolet, and Mercedes to build the affordable 190 SL to complement the high-end 300 SL. He told BMW he could sell a top-flight roadster for no more than $4,500 retail, at which price he promised a "firm order of 1,000 cars," projecting annual sales of 3,000 to 4,000 cars in the US.

In its initial planning, however, BMW had conceived the roadster's production on an entirely different scale: as a hand-built car sold in Europe by the hundreds, not thousands. Crafting the car's aluminum bodywork took some 600 hours, making it impossible to deliver the 507 at the price Hoffman wanted, or in the volumes he imagined.

Despite that reality, and even though BMW already had a US importer—the Fadex Corporation owned by Fred Oppenheimer—BMW continued to move forward with the 507 based on Hoffman's promises.

The 507 was hailed for its beauty at Frankfurt, but its commercial success in still-recovering Europe was by no means certain. In early 1957, board member for sales Ernst Hof encouraged the arrangement with Hoffman as a means of penetrating the giant US market with a high-end automobile. As BMW's board meeting minutes reveal, Hof also warned that Hoffman was "an exceptionally savvy importer and vendor, as well as a wealthy businessman" who would require "exact contractual arrangements."

By then, as the BMW board was certainly aware, Mercedes had followed Jaguar in terminating its contract with Hoffman, paying

Albrecht Graf von Goertz, who designed the 507 and 503 for BMW on Max Hoffman's recommendation.

$2.55 million to do so a full year prior to its expiration. Mercedes cited Hoffman's failure to provide adequate after-sales service and spare parts to customers, but it was also losing money on the cars it sold in the US, in particular the low-priced models commissioned by Hoffman.

Despite all of that, BMW began to plan 507 production and sales based on Hoffman's initial order estimate of 5,000 cars in total. The company was left in the lurch when Hoffman downgraded that number to 1,500, and finally to 1,200, just 300 per year over four years.

In relaying the story to Ludvigsen in 1972, Hoffman omitted all but the first figure: "I placed an order for 5,000 cars, but they couldn't build them. They had no factory at that time; they didn't tool up for them."

Hoffman neglected to mention that tooling up for series production was contingent on a $500,000 prepayment that he failed to make.

The details of the 507 debacle were investigated by former BMW engine chief Dr. Karlheinz Lange and reported in his seminal book, *The legendary BMW 507*, published by BMW Mobile Tradition in 2005.

As Lange reports, the first production 507 wasn't built until December 1956, and only 19 cars had been built through March 1957, including the first Series II cars built with the additional legroom and other features demanded by Hoffman for the US.

"In April, negotiations still had not reached a satisfactory conclusion," Lange writes. "Hoffman kept introducing new conditions and options into the discussions. To complicate matters, Fadex also expressed interest in importing the complete BMW range, and Fadex was prepared to pay higher prices than Hoffman."

Max Hoffman never sold BMW's small cars in the US. Instead, the Isettas, 600s, and 700s were sold by Fred Oppenheimer's Fadex corporation, which had its showroom at 487 Park Avenue in New York City…just up the street from Hoffman's at 375 Park Avenue. (Below, left) Cary Grant poses with an Isetta for a Fadex publicity photo. (Right) A Fadex ad for the 700 coupe.

Despite the confusion, the BMW board gave the go-ahead for production of the 507 in May 1957, with a plan to build 1,000 examples in 1958. That month, as Lange notes, BMW chairman Richter-Brohm requested order forecasts from BMW dealers for the first time. When German dealers placed orders for just 60-70 507s, BMW terminated its large-scale production plans for the roadster. Once a "stock order" for 100 cars had been fulfilled, the car would be discontinued. Negotiations with Hoffman were still ongoing, however, and the board reserved the right to make a separate decision on an additional 2,000 cars for the US.

By then, Hoffman had taken delivery of just 15 507s; in 1958, he ordered only one more.

That September, BMW restored sole US distribution to Oppenheimer's Fadex, which had retained the rights to sell the sub-1.0- liter cars and had sold 8,872 Isettas in 1957. (Hoffman was never involved with Isetta sales in the US.) The novelty of BMW's egg-shaped microcar had worn off by 1958, when only 1,531 Isettas crossed the Atlantic, but the 600 and 700 picked up part of the slack, selling in combined volumes of 2,039 and 1,024 cars in 1958 and '59. In 1960, Fadex could shift only 100 Isettas and 875 of the larger 700s, and in 1961—the last year of Oppenheimer's contract—total US imports fell to just 232 cars, all but two of which were 700s.

Oppenheimer sold a small number of V8-powered Baroque Angels, 503s, and 507s, doing so in parallel with Max Hoffman from 1956 to 1958, but those cars would never have the mass appeal needed to crack the American market. The New Class might have done it in 1963, and the 1600-2 certainly did in 1966, but Oppenheimer never got the chance to offer those vehicles. When his contract expired in 1961, BMW didn't renew it, citing his inability to turn Fadex into the national sales network that BMW needed. (Oppenheimer was already representing NSU, and he'd do so until that brand's absorption into Volkswagen in the late 1960s.)

BMW explored the possibility of setting up its own sales subsidiary, but its resources were already stretched too thin. In 1962, it awarded its US import contract to none other than Max Hoffman, citing the strength of his financial position and his extensive dealer network.

Far more important, perhaps, was Hoffman's personal relationship with Paul Hahnemann, recently appointed to the BMW board as a deputy member in charge of sales worldwide.

As Ludvigsen noted in his *Bimmer* article of 1998, "Hahnemann was not averse to arrangements that enriched him privately, and Hoffman was a man of the world. They got along well."

Hoffman's ad for the New Class 1500 and 1800 sedans of 1965. He'd sell 952 of the four-door cars that year, and a total of 2,216 through 1970.

It would take a few years for either man to be enriched. In 1962, its first year of the renewed Hoffman contract, BMW exported just 720 cars to the US. 1963 was even worse, with just 211 cars reaching this country. Sales of the New Class started picking up in 1964, but even then BMW exported just 786 cars to the US. As we've already seen, 1965 and '66 saw exports of 1,230 and 1,253 cars, respectively, making BMW a minuscule player indeed in the 9 million-car US auto market.

All of that changed with the arrival of the 1600-2, yet even the 4,564 cars exported to the US in 1967 seemed like a fraction of what was possible. A more powerful car would have more appeal in this market, as Hoffman surely knew.

In "The Baron of Park Avenue," Hoffman claimed that he'd advocated for the installation of the 2.0-liter engine in the Type 114 two-door but was told by BMW executives that it wouldn't fit. Hoffman said he insisted that it would, threatening to take a 2.0-liter engine to Schorsch Meier's dealership and have Meier install it in a 1600-2 chassis. At that point, Hoffman said, BMW relented and the 2002 was born.

No documents within the BMW Archive confirm that account, and Archive historians dispute it.

"Absolutely not!" says Fred Jakobs. "Schorsch Meier was very settled in his BMW dealership, and he would never work against the company. He wasn't an idiot."

Moreover, Hoffman's claim is *prima facie* absurd. No one within BMW would have told Hoffman the engine wouldn't fit, because the M10's external dimensions were the same regardless of internal displacement.

Jakobs' fellow Archive historian Dr. Annika Biss suggests it doesn't really matter, noting that Hoffman's reputation within BMW had taken an irreparable hit in the late 1950s.

"After the 507, his opinion was nonsense," says Dr. Biss. "He lost influence. If BMW trusted him any more, I would be surprised."

Paul Hahnemann notwithstanding.

The *real* origins of the 2002

If not at Hoffman's urging, how *did* the 1600-2 end up being fitted with a 2.0-liter engine?

Reviewing the 2002 for *Car and Driver* in April 1968, David E. Davis Jr. said it happened organically, calling the move "pure BMW."

"The current 2000 series [the New Class sedan] started life in 1962 as a 1500, then it became an 1800 and finally a full two liters—going from 94 to 114 horsepower in the process," Davis wrote. "The current 1600 was introduced about a year and a half ago, and BMW-philes everywhere began to think of that glorious day in the future when the factory would decide to put in the 2-liter engine."

Indeed, it was probably inevitable that BMW would expand the Type 114 lineup with larger-displacement engines, just as it had the New Class sedan.

As we've already learned, the M10 four-cylinder had been engineered to allow for easy displacement increases. While the engine was under development, engine chief Alexander von Falkenhausen (**opposite, in 1966, attempting to set a world speed record with a BMW-powered Brabham F2 car**) had argued strenuously for a crankshaft with five main bearings instead of three, which would allow the engine to make more power with no loss of reliability.

Just as importantly, Karl Rech had designed the M10's robust cast-iron block with cylinder spacing of 93mm, allowing the block to be bored out significantly while still leaving enough metal around the water passages between each cylinder.

In its original 1.5-liter configuration, the M10 had oversquare dimensions of 82 x 71mm. Enlarged in 1963 to 1.8 liters, both its bore and stroke increased (to 84 x 80mm, for 1,773cc). For the 1.6-liter version of 1964, only the bore was increased (84 x 71mm, for 1,573cc).

Though it might seem counterintuitive that BMW would build the smaller of those two engines after having already enlarged the engine to 1.8 liters, the answer lies in motorsport. Von Falkenhausen was a racer to his core, and he engineered BMW's motors to take advantage of the rulebook in any series that would be suitable to BMW's products.

Paul Hahnemann, by contrast, was largely indifferent to racing except as a marketing tool. As mentioned earlier, Hahnemann had advocated for the use of the 1.6-liter engine in BMW's new two-door to give the car a tie-in to Formula 2. As the 1600-2 was under development, so were BMW's F2 engines. Equally important, the factory team was beginning to enter its New Class sedans in FIA Group 2 racing for "improved production cars" produced in volumes of at least 1,000 units.

In 1964, BMW entered its factory 1800 TI—for *Turismo Internationale*—in the 24 Hours of Spa. Despite competing against cars with engines displacing up to 3.0 liters, the 1800 TI was competitive in Group 2 thanks to the 110-hp output of its 1,773cc engine, along with other performance-minded improvements. The car won its class, and it nearly won the race; driver Rauno Aaltonen thinks its second-place overall to a larger Mercedes came down to a scoring error.

The 1800 TI was BMW's first truly race-worthy car since the 328, and its success spurred BMW to create a privateer racing version for 1965: the 1800 TI/SA, an Italian-German acronym for *Turismo Internationale Sonder Ausfuhring*, or Touring International Special Performance.

US importer Max Hoffman imported 54 examples of the 1800 TI/SA—one quarter of total production—to the US in 1965, and he claimed to have commissioned the car's creation. That can't be verified, but it's highly unlikely even though Hoffman was a racer himself in his youth and in his early days as a Porsche importer in the late '40s and early '50s. In any event, his importation of these exotic racers helped raise BMW's profile in the US when a handful of drivers entered them in the popular SCCA Trans-Am series.

In 1966, BMW's factory team moved on to the 2000 sedan, whose 1,990cc engine took full advantage of 1965's new Group 2 displacement regulations. The new rules divided cars into three divisions and five-sub-groups: Division 1 for cars of 0-850cc and 851-1,000cc; Division 2 for cars of 1,001-1,300cc, 1,301-1,600cc, and 1,601-2,000cc; and Division 3 for cars with over 2,000cc. The classifications changed slight for 1966, when Division 2 was limited to the two smaller-displacement sub-groups (1,300cc and 1,600cc) and Division 3 was limited to cars from 1,600cc to 2,000cc.

BMW raced its 2000 TI sedan for the first time at the Nürburgring on July 3, 1966, a few months after the launch of the 1600-2 and just

BMW celebrated its class victory at Spa '64 with "win ads" in European magazines.

two days before BMW started discussing a 2.0-liter engine for the Type 114 two-door.

On July 5, 1966, the BMW board of management agreed that a 2.0-liter version of the Type 114 would be suitable. Development funds were tight, however, and the board—now led by Gerhard Wilcke, a Quandt Group lawyer who'd taken over following the surprise departure of Dr. Karl-Heinz Sonne in 1965—felt that the larger engine would require additional changes that would become too expensive. They agreed to revisit the situation a year later.

More immediately, they decided to create a higher-performance "TI" version of the 1600, which Hahnemann felt would succeed thanks to its connection with BMW's new F2 engine, set to debut in 1967. (After winning the 1966 European Touring Car Championship with Hubert Hahne and the 2000 TI, BMW would turn its attention to Formula 2 exclusively for 1967.)

Neither engine chief von Falkenhausen nor planning director Helmut-Werner Bönsch waited for board approval before installing the 2.0-liter engine in their personal 1600-2s. As reported in 1998's *The cult car* (the official history of the 2002 published by BMW Mobile Tradition, now BMW Classic), both men did so independently in early 1967. They probably had a good laugh when they discovered that the other had done the same.

Like von Falkenhausen, Bönsch was a strong technician, and a capable strategist. Joining BMW in 1958 from Kronprinz Wheels—he'd also worked as an engineer for Siemens, Shell, and Mannesmann Steel—he was charged with value analysis and quality control from the engineering side. He'd pushed BMW to build a 700 sedan as a more practical offering alongside the stylish 700 coupe. When BMW bought Glas, Bönsch was charged with bringing its products up to BMW standards, and with transforming the 1300 GT into the BMW 1600 GT, incorporating the best of both companies' engineering.

Von Falkenhausen and Bönsch agreed to present their hot rods to Hahnemann, hoping to get his approval for a series production model. After trying one out for himself, Hahnemann was convinced.

While that was happening in Munich, a Minnesotan named Glen Dye was nearing the end of an 18-month tour of duty in Germany with the US armed forces. Like so many US service members, he'd been turned on to BMW performance while stationed overseas, and he'd also become aware that Alpina could deliver BMW hot rods that were even better than stock.

According to an article in *Car and Driver*'s December 1967 issue, Dye went to Alpina in its original home of Kaufbeuren—the firm hadn't yet moved to Buchloe—and ordered a 1600-2 with a high-performance 2.0-liter

Car and Driver tested Glen Dye's Alpina-built 2.0-liter 1600 two-door over Labor Day weekend in 1967, publishing its report in December 1967.

Alpina engine in place of the standard 85-hp 1.6-liter. He waited seven months for the car to be completed, then brought it home to the US and let the magazine test it over Labor Day weekend, 1967.

Car and Driver reported Dye's "intoxication" with his car's performance. His car had been fitted with a 2.0-liter engine sourced from the 2000 TI sedan that delivered a reported 135 SAE hp. (BMW claimed 120 DIN hp for the 2000 TI.) Upgraded by Alpina with 45mm Weber carbs, a more aggressive camshaft, increased compression (from 9.3 to 10.5:1), and Alpina exhaust headers, the engine produced an impressive 160 hp at 6,900 rpm and 135 lb-ft at 5,250 rpm.

The magazine was disappointed that Alpina had retained the 6-volt electrical system, but that inadequacy was quickly forgotten in light of the car's five-speed manual transmission, limited slip differential, 10.25-inch ventilated front disc brakes, 165-13 Michelin XAS tires, adjustable Koni shocks, and Alpina anti-roll bars.

"We just couldn't resist putting down the guys in their hopped-up, middle-aged Chevys and the like. But if the hot-rodders were chagrined, the sports car types were overwhelmed. In one day on Long Island, we must have destroyed the egos of at least half a dozen unsuspecting owners of Triumphs, MGs, and Alfa Romeos."

No doubt they did. In measured testing, Dye's 2,391-lb. Alpina ran the zero-to-60 sprint in just 8.3 seconds, genuinely quick for 1967. More impressive still was the car's handling. *Car and Driver* said its testers "have seldom driven a car which is as confidence-inspiring on twisty roads," which surely helped Dye justify spending $5,048.45 at Alpina, plus another $531 to get his car to the US. That was twice as much as a new 1600-2 from Hoffman, but it was arguably a small price to pay for such stirring performance…and for a car that was far ahead of anything BMW

The twin-carburetor, 105-hp (DIN) 1600 TI, introduced in 1967.

was planning to build.

The timeline presented in *Car and Driver* means that Dye would have ordered his car no later than February 1967, at about the same time that von Falkenhausen and Bönsch were building their own 2.0-liter two-doors, but well before the BMW board had approved production for a 2.0-liter Type 114.

Asked whether Alpina had been building a 2.0-liter Type 114 before BMW, Alpina founder Burkard Bovensiepen was emphatic. "Not true at all," he said. Bovensiepen doesn't remember Dye's car, but he concurs with David E. Davis Jr. that a 2.0-liter version was inevitable, to suit racing's practicalities as well as market demand. "When the 1602 was born, it was a normal development that it would be a 2.0-liter car," Bovensiepen said.

In mid-September 1967, a few weeks after *Car and Driver* tested Dye's car in New York, BMW presented the 1600 TI at Frankfurt.

Like its TI counterparts among the New Class sedans, the two-door 1600 TI was a sportier version that offered customers improved performance while giving BMW a more competitive platform in touring car racing, which required the homologation of standard parts.

The TI's sporting improvements began with the 1,573cc engine. Von Falkenhausen's team increased compression from 8.6 to 9.5:1, then replaced the 1600-2's single Solex 38 PDSI carburetor with two Solex 40 PHH carburetors. So modified, output increased from 85 horsepower at 5,700 rpm/93 lb-ft at 3,000 rpm to 105 hp at 6,000 rpm/98.6 lb-ft at 4,500 rpm. With a lower rear axle ratio (3.9 vs. 4.11:1), the 1600 TI could scoot from zero to 62 mph in just 11.5 seconds, significantly faster than the 13.3 seconds needed by the 1600-2.

To improve handling, the TI got anti-roll bars at both axles. Its 240mm front discs and 200mm rear drum brakes were the same diameter as those on the standard 1600-2, but the TI featured

The 1600 TI interior got a sportier three-spoke steering wheel and a tachometer. (Earliest models had "silver dollar" gauge faces.)

power assist that made hard braking easier.

To sportify the car's appearance, BMW gave the TI a grille with a "1600 ti" badge and horizontal slats finished in matte black, but for two in the center that remained bright metal. In the cockpit, the TI was equipped with a tachometer and a sportier three-spoke steering wheel.

The 1600 TI represented the last word in Type 114 performance for 1967, but it remained inaccessible to US enthusiasts, who were already clamoring for a more powerful version of BMW's new two-door. The twin-carb TI motor simply didn't run clean enough to satisfy US emissions regulations.

Industrial and automobile-related pollution—"smog"—had been recognized as a problem in the US since the late 1940s. By the early 1960s, the situation was particularly acute in the Los Angeles basin, where pollution reached eye-irritating levels on 212 of 365 days in 1962. Los Angeles had already banned the use of coal and oil as industrial fuel, and by 1963 the state of California was regulating automotive emissions. First, the state required crankcase return valves, and in 1966 exhaust emissions controls were added to the list of mandated equipment.

On the federal level, the 1963 Clean Air Act gave the US government limited ability to regulate interstate pollution, and the 1965 Motor Vehicle Air Pollution Act brought national standards in line with California's for the 1968 model year. In the meantime, the 1967 Air

Quality Act had been enacted to control lead emissions, while hydrocarbon emissions were regulated on the federal level from 1968. Cars displacing less than 100 cubic inches (1,639cc) were permitted emissions measured at 410 ppm of unburned hydrocarbons and 2.3% carbon monoxide, while those displacing 100-140 cubic inches (1,639-2,294cc) were only allowed 350 ppm of hydrocarbons and 2.0% carbon monoxide.

European countries including Germany had yet to begin regulating vehicle emissions—the Euro 1 standard wouldn't come into effect until 1992—but the importance of the US market meant that manufacturers were forced to take US regulations into account nonetheless.

Throughout the 1960s, emissions regulations loom large in BMW's discussions around US-market cars. At the board meeting of August 9, 1967, development/production chief Gieschen reported that the US-spec 1600-2 would be equipped with "exhaust detoxification" as of August 23 production. Performance would suffer slightly, he said—*Road & Track* reported a noticeable difference—and the car's retail price would increase by $100.

Cleaner-running cars were all well and good, but US enthusiasts were chafing at the unavailability of the 1600 TI. The car's absence from the US was lamented by David E. Davis in the same issue of *Car and Driver* that featured Glen Dye's hot-rod Alpina.

Writing after the Frankfurt auto show in September, Davis said that "BMW can't seem to make their smog control air-pump work on multi-carburetor engines, making [the 1600 TI] illegal here after the first of the year.

"Being denied the 1600 TI is a calamity to rival the Johnstown Flood for sheer awfulness. The 1600 TI *has* to be the greatest thing to come out of Germany since Marlene Dietrich."

With the high-performance TI off-limits, BMW needed a car that would satisfy the desire of US enthusiasts for more power in a compact two-door package.

The solution was obvious: Put the single-carb 2.0-liter engine into the Type 114 chassis.

In addition to "exhaust detoxification" for the US-spec 1600-2, the minutes from BMW's August 9 board meeting mention the 2.0-liter Type 114 that Hahnemann had already driven: "At the suggestion of Herr Hahnemann, the board decides to equip the 1600-2 for the USA with a 2-liter engine for an additional price of another $100. This version is intended as a replacement for the omitted 2-liter model and the TIS version. The associated investment costs are from [production director Bernhard] Osswald priced at approximately DM 200,000 ($50,000). Start as fast as possible."

Two weeks later, on August 22, 1967, the board discusses the car again, this time deciding to build the new 2.0-liter car not as a pure sports model like the 1600 TI, but as one whose "buying circles" would be different. Again, the board mentions the need to build the 2.0-liter car because the 1600 TI can't be "detoxified." Six days later the 2.0-liter two-door was confirmed for production.

By October 24, 1967, the new model had a name, 2002, which referenced both its engine displacement and its two-door body style without the hyphenation that had encumbered the 1600-2. To rationalize the nomenclature, the earlier model would become the 1602, but that change wouldn't be formalized until 1971.

Production of the home-market 2002 began in January 1968, and the car went on sale in Germany for DM 9,394 ($2,349). Indicative of the US market's role in its creation—and importance to its success—production of a US-spec 2002 began just one month later.

By the end of the year, demand was far outstripping supply, and customers were forced to wait several months to purchase a 2002. After trying for more than a decade to crack the US market, BMW had finally done it.

So who deserves credit for a car that became one of the best-loved BMWs of all time?

Probably not US importer Max Hoffman, who claimed that the 2002 had been built at his insistence, and over BMW's objections.

"If you asked him, of course he would say so," says the BMW Archive's Dr. Biss.

Hoffman surely wanted a more powerful two-door for the US market, yet none of the BMW Board of Management's discussions mention his name; throughout, US emissions standards are cited as the driving factor behind the 2.0-liter Type 114. David E. Davis confirmed as much in Car and Driver, writing in April 1968 that the 2002 "was originally proposed as a kind of second-choice, American anti-smog version of the wailing 1600 TI they were selling in Germany."

More likely, no individual deserves full credit. Alpina's Burkard Bovensiepen had already built at least one 2.0-liter Type 114 on customer demand. BMW engineers Alex von Falkenhausen and Helmut-Werner Bönsch did so themselves, proving the concept at the OEM level. Sales chief Paul Hahnemann advocated for it on the board of management, where chairman Gerhard Wilcke (**below, with the 2002**) approved it. Some credit should go to the federal regulators whose emissions standards barred the 1600 TI from the US; otherwise, we might have gotten a twin-carb 1600 rather than one with a larger engine.

Instead, we got the 2002, the car that changed everything for BMW in the US.

Gerhard Wilcke, BMW chairman from December 1966 to the end of 1969, with a 2002.

Type 114, or E10?

BMW enthusiasts have long debated whether the 2002 is rightly designated as a Type 114 or an E10. The confusion stems from BMW's shift to a new ordering sequence in the 1960s, when it ceased to assign three-digit type numbers and began using a new series of *Entwicklung*, German for "development," codes.

The change from type numbers to E-codes was initiated by Bernhard Osswald (**at far right in photo opposite, with Gerhard Wilcke, Paul Hahnemann, and an unidentified journalist**) after his arrival at BMW from Volkswagen on January 1, 1965. Osswald joined the board as a deputy member in charge of development, and he was made a full member on December 1, 1965.

Osswald's new sequence effectively started over, replacing the type numbers that had been in use since at least 1933. BMW's prewar cars had been assigned type numbers in the 300s, which coincided with their model designations.

After the war, BMW's first cars were large sedans, conceived as an extension of its prewar developments in the same category. Those cars were assigned type numbers and model designations in the 500s, but the two numbers don't always coincide.

When BMW began building small cars, it assigned them a new sequence of numbers beginning with 100. The cars that went into production are as follows:

100: Isetta
102: 600
107: 700 coupe
107S: 700 Sport
110: Baur-built 700 cabriolet
111: 700 sedan
114: Small midsize car, 1300/1500cc, developed further to build series '02
115: First New Class sedan, 1500
116: New Class sedan, 1600

2002: A Development History 53

118: New Class sedan, 1800
119: 700 LS
120: 2000 C/CS coupe
121: New Class sedan, 2000

It's important to note that BMW didn't yet refer to any project as an *Entwicklung*, and that none of these numbers should be preceded by the letter E. Instead, the projects are referred to as "types," and all internal documents reference them as such, i.e. Type 114.

It's equally important to note that BMW has never circulated an official list of its type designations or E-codes, not even internally. Some have been confirmed, however, including all of the Types and E-codes used herein.

Instituted at some point after Osswald's arrival in 1965, the E-codes begat a new sequence, beginning with E1. Both E1 and E2 went unassigned, saved for later but presumably never used. The first production car assigned an E-code is the E3 sedan, which was probably designated as a Type 122 during the initial development process.

The first car of the Type 114 body style to recive an E-code was the Touring. Originally designated the 114K, it was assigned E6 during its long gestation. The second was the battery-powered 1600-2, and the third was the 2.0-liter Type 114, aka the 2002.

The 2002 was designated E10, though that code wasn't assigned by the BMW board on August 28, 1967, when the decision was made to build the Type 114 with a 2.0-liter engine. Instead, the car is referred to as a "2.0-liter Type 114" during those initial discussions, with the E-code applied after the car was approved for production—perhaps as late as 1969, the start date for the electric E7 project that precedes it numerically.

The exact date of the changeover can't be determined at this writing, though additional research might reveal further information. In any case, BMW's early E-code sequence for its production cars is as follows:

E3: Large sedan
E6: Touring version of the Type 114, originally designated Type 114K
E7: Battery-powered Type 114 used in the 1972 Olympics
E9: Large coupe with six-cylinder engine, successor to the 2000 C/CS
E10: Small build series '02' with 2-liter motor, production from 1968
E10/C: Baur Cabrio
E10/T: Project Turbo, later assigned the development code **E20**
E10/73: Square-taillight update to the 2002 for the 1974 model year.

Note that the E10 designation was applied primarily if not exclusively to cars with the 2.0-liter engine. By all accounts, the Type 114 designation continued to apply to the smaller-engined two-doors (the 1600-2/1602, and presumably the 1802 and 1502) throughout their lifespan.

Going forward, we'll continue to refer to the body style in general as the Type 114, and to individual models by their specific E-code where appropriate.

Turn Your Hymnals to 2002— David E. Davis, Jr. Blows His Mind on the Latest from BMW

BMW drops the Whispering Bomb

If the 1600-2 caused a stir, the 2002 created a sensation. Arriving in 1968, the car carried a retail price of $2,988. For an additional $258 premium over the 1600-2, customers got an outwardly similar two-door sedan powered by a 1,990cc four-cylinder engine rather than one displacing 1,573cc.

Along with an 89 x 80mm bore and stroke, the larger engine featured a crankshaft with eight counterweights instead of four. With 8.5:1 compression and a single Solex 40 PDSI downdraft carburetor, the engine's output was rated at 113 hp (SAE) at 5,800 rpm and 115.7 lb-ft at 3,000 rpm. The additional 17 horsepower and 24.7 lb-ft of torque helped the 2002 achieve a higher top speed (106 vs. 100 mph) and a faster zero-to-60 mph time (11.5 vs. 13.3 seconds) than the 1600-2 despite being 52 lbs. heavier. (BMW claimed a curb weight of 2,080 lbs., while *Road & Track* noted a curb weight of 2,210 lbs. and a test weight of 2,565 lbs. for the 2002.)

A four-speed manual transmission was standard, with a three-speed automatic available as an extra-cost option; either was followed by a differential equipped with a taller final drive ratio (3.64 rather than 4.11:1).

Both cars used 240mm front disk brakes, but the 2002 got rear drum brakes that measured 230mm where the 1600-2's were 200mm. Power assist was standard—a $45 "mandatory option" from Hoffman—but *Road & Track* deemed braking effort "rather heavy," nonetheless, and braking performance "not outstanding, but acceptable and with excellent control."

The 2002's four-wheel independent suspension was bolstered by anti-roll bars at both ends, while its springs and dampers were stiffer than the 1600-2's "in anticipation of more vigorous driving," according to *Road & Track*'s first drive report from Germany.

The car did indeed inspire vigorous driving… and an ecstatic review from *Car and Driver* editor David E. Davis Jr. in April 1968.

In "Turn Your Hymnals to 2002," Davis explained that "the 2002 is BMW's way of coping with the smog problem. They couldn't import their little 1600 TI, so the stuffed in the smooth, quiet 2.0-liter engine from the larger 2000 sedan and—SHAZAM—instant winner!"

After praising its interior comforts and civility, Davis goes on to offer a thoroughly gonzo description of the 2002's performance.

"The minute it starts moving, you know that Fangio and Moss and Tony Brooks and all those other big racing studs retired only because they feared that someday you'd have one of these, and when that day came, you'd be indomitable. They were right. You are indomitable."

Davis goes on to blow off a Plymouth, Mustang, Austin-Healey and a GTO before training his sights on Triumphs and Porsches to "slaughter, no matter how hard they try. They really believe all that jazz about their highly-tuned, super-sophisticated sports machines, and the first couple of drubbings at the hands of the 2002 make them think they're off on a bad trip or something. But then they learn the awful truth, and they begin to hang back at traffic signals, pretending they weren't really racing at all. Ha! Grovel, Morgan. Slink home with your tail between your legs, MG-B. Hide in the garage when you see a BMW coming."

The 2002 was fast, as Davis noted, but it was also much more. "It rides like a dream. It has a surprising amount of room inside. It gets great gas mileage. It's finished, inside and out, like a Mercedes-Benz, but it doesn't cost very much."

With aggressive ads for the 2002, the Harvey agency created a powerful image for BMW as "The Sportsman's Car," and for the BMW customer as a passionate enthusiast of driving.

He had only one real complaint about the car he called "most certainly the best $2,850 sedan in the whole cotton-picking world," and that was with a Blaupunkt radio that "couldn't pick up a Manhattan station from the far end of the Brooklyn Bridge." That line caused Blaupunkt to pull its advertising from *Car and Driver*, and it got Davis fired as a senior editor at the magazine.

By then, Davis' column had already sent countless enthusiasts to BMW dealers, eager to check out what Davis called "one of modern civilization's all-time best ways to get somewhere sitting down."

Reviews like Davis's helped cement BMW's identity as a sporty marque in the US, as did new ads by the James Neal Harvey agency for Hoffman Motors Corporation.

Having created clever, innovative ads for the 1600-2, Harvey took it a step further with the arrival of the 2002. A 1968 ad featuring both Type 114 models identified them not as the 1600-2 and 2002 but as "Fast" and "Faster than Fast." The new 2002 was proclaimed "the same beautifully-crafted sedan as the 1600, with one exception. It mounts our big, hairy-chested 2.0-liter engine." Alongside the roundel, it proclaims BMW "The Sportsman's Car."

While defining the BMW car, Harvey's ads also defined the BMW *driver*: passionate, sophisticated, eager to experience exhilarating performance but sensible enough to want good value and a high-quality automobile. He—and it was always a he—was the kind of man anyone would want to be, making a BMW the kind of car anyone would like to own, should they be so discerning.

Between praise from the press and persuasive advertising—not to mention word-of-mouth from early buyers eager to tell everyone they met about their fabulous new 2002s—BMW's US exports rose from 4,564 cars in 1967 to 9,172 in 1968; of those, 5,236 were 1600-2s and 3,892 were 2002s. The remaining 44 cars

consisted of twenty 2000 sedans and thirteen 2000 CS coupes, both powered by the 2.0-liter four-cylinder M10 engine. Hoffman also imported six 2500 sedans, the first cars of larger E3 body style featuring the new 2.5-liter M30 six-cylinder engine.

The 1600-2 and 2002 would remain BMW's strongest sellers in this market even after the arrival in 1969 of the gorgeous E9 2800 CS coupe. The six-cylinder E3 sedans and E9 coupes were far more expensive than their four-cylinder counterparts—the 2500 carried a retail price of roughly $5,000, while the 2800 CS went for around $8,000—and they sold in relatively small quantities as a result. In 1969, BMW exported 1,225 of its E3 sedans (2500 and 2800) to the US, along with 62 2800 CS coupes and a single 2000 CS.

The Type 114s, meanwhile, continued to soar in popularity through 1969, with US enthusiasts snapping up 2,675 of the 1600-2s and 6,962 of the 2002s that year. In accordance with new US safety standards, all BMWs were now equipped with dual-circuit brakes, seat belts, side lamps, and bumper protectors, plus the mandatory equipment like headrests and 12-volt electrics added to the US-spec 1600-2 in 1967. (BMW was a little late to adopt dual-circuit brakes, fitting them to the 2002 starting in July 1968 and to the 1600-2 in February 1969 even though the US federal government had mandated them from January 1, 1968.) Hoffman continued to import the New Class sedan, and 713 examples of the 1800 and 2000 sedan brought 1969's export total to 11,638.

Those increases meant that the US was finally becoming a significant market for BMW, consuming an ever-larger share of Munich's production. In 1966, US exports had accounted for just 1.7% of BMW's production of 74,075 cars; a year later, the US took 5.2% of the 87,618 automobiles produced in Munich. In 1968 and

BMW press photos show the 2002 on the streets of Munich in 1968.

1969, BMW exported 7.9% of its production of 116,547 and 147,851 automobiles to the US, helping global exports rise to 40% of total production in those years.

Within the giant US market, however, BMW remained minuscule. From 1966 through 1969, some 8.3 to 9.6 million new cars were sold in the US each year, of which BMW's share represented 0.01, 0.05, 0.09, and 0.12 percent of the total.

On the basis of those increases, Max Hoffman requested a new import contract on December 5, 1969. In 1970, Hahnemann agreed on behalf of BMW to grant Hoffman a 12-year contract to represent BMW in the US, with an automatic six-year extension (through 1988) if Hoffman built a suitable import center in New Jersey.

In an industry where five-year contracts were standard, it was an unusually long-term deal, and it would have serious ramifications a few years later.

Before we explore those ramifications, let's find out who was buying new BMWs in this country, the enthusiasts who took a chance on a virtually unknown automobile.

Many came to the marque after reading David E. Davis Jr. in *Car and Driver*, which tended to attract a somewhat nonconformist reader. Where *Motor Trend* served the daily driver and *Road & Track* catered to the gentleman enthusiast of European sports cars and Grands Prix racing, *Car and Driver* took a more counter-cultural perspective from its offices at One Park Avenue in New York City. With Leon Mandel as editor in chief, the magazine was brash and literate. The same issue in which Davis raved about the 2002 found Brock Yates describing *Reader's Digest* as "a pleasant diet of soft-core fascism," calling that magazine "a clarion call for the American Gothic way of life."

Car and Driver readers were looking for something far more exciting, and they weren't afraid to gamble on an obscure Bavarian

automobile in search of the perfect combination of handling, speed, and practicality. In "Turn Your Hymnals to 2002," Davis had described exactly what they were looking for.

"If you read that and your blood doesn't start boiling a bit, get *Reader's Digest* and call it a day. It's Biblical," says Michael Izor, then a junior accountant with a media company in Boston. "I was one of those American car guys, and here comes this pocket rocket that just sounds fabulous. I went to the local dealership and asked for a test drive, and I was so impressed I placed an order."

So did newly-minted college graduate Rob Mitchell. "I'd dreamed since day one of owning something interesting, but I was a second lieutenant in the Marine Corps making $6,000 a year, so I had to dream affordably," Mitchell recalls. "When the April '68 *Car and Driver* showed up in my mailbox, the 2002 sounded like the answer to my prayers. Six months earlier, I couldn't have told you what BMW was." After buying his 1600-2, Mitchell started selling BMWs at Foreign Motors West in Natick, Massachusetts, and he'd go on to spend a long career working for BMW of North America.

"Turn Your Hymnals" persuaded Los Angeles' Roger Scilley to trade his Opel Kadett for a 2002, and Doug Shirachi to order one with the earnings from his first aerospace engineering job. It convinced Jim Craig to buy a BMW instead of a Porsche when he graduated from Virginia Tech. It got Boston broadcaster Bob Mehrman to part with the Triumph TR3 he'd been rallying with the Touring Club of New England.

Similar stories were unfolding all over the country, and it wasn't long before enthusiasts began banding together to share their fascination for BMW's splendid little coupe. In 1969 and 1970, BMW clubs formed in Boston, at Stanford University, in Ohio, in Kansas City, in Seattle, in Chicago, and in Los Angeles.

The Boston club was one of the first, created by Mehrman and early 1600-2 enthusiast Michel Potheau in the spring of 1969. Their BMW Car Club of America quickly went national, incorporating the other clubs as chapters of the larger organization. Eventually, even the Hoffman-sanctioned, Los Angeles-based BMW Automobile Club of America came under the CCA umbrella.

Regardless of the structure under which they organized, early car club members shared more than just their affection for BMW. They also shared information. Early CCA member (and English teacher) Joseph Chamberlain says the club was at heart "a self-preservation society.

"BMWs were significantly better than domestic products, but compared to modern autos they were terrible shitboxes," Chamberlain says. "Anyone who owned a 2002 constantly replaced stuff. If you got 40,000 miles on a water pump it was a miracle, and if you got three or four years on a fan belt or radiator hose, that was really something. We didn't think anything of it, because a lot of us were coming from British cars that spent more time in the garage than being driven. By comparison, the BMWs were tremendous."

Parts prices from Hoffman were high, however, so the club newsletters published suggestions for cheaper alternatives. The same Hella relay for which a BMW dealer charged $11, for example, was only $5 from a Volkswagen dealer.

Worse, perhaps, many BMW dealers were woefully under-informed about the marque. The bar to entry was low—prospective dealers had to pay around $1,500 for a franchise and to place an initial order for just three cars—and by 1967 Hoffman and his six sub-distributors had established a network of 129 dealers in 29 states. Most had been independent repair shops before morphing into BMW dealerships, and the best were run by recent immigrants from Germany who brought technical expertise and familiarity with the brand. Unfortunately, many more were run by people who had limited knowledge of the cars they were selling.

Given Hoffman's reluctance to provide technical information or sales training, that left many owners to their own devices when it came to maintaining their BMWs. The clubs filled the gap, to the extent that it was possible, but the situation was far from ideal.

If ordinary customers were largely on their own when it came to technical matters, racers in the US were doubly so, receiving no support from Hoffman. Nonetheless, the handling and performance that attracted enthusiasts to the Type 114 made the cars ideal for racing, at least on some US circuits.

A few drivers had raced 1600-2s, but the cars' 1.6-liter engines put them at a displacement disadvantage in the SCCA's Trans-Am series' Under 2-liter class. Running competitively meant stepping up to a 2002 when that car arrived in 1968, but even then, the BMW suffered from the same power deficit it faced in Europe against the Alfa GTAs and Porsche 911s.

In 1970, when new SCCA rules forced the 911 to move up a class, the 2002 was suddenly in the hunt. At Loudon, New Hampshire that May, Peter Schuster took the 2002's first Trans-Am win. Sponsored by Bavarian Auto Sales of Long Island City, New York, Schuster put his BMW on the podium in four races that season, but he DNF'd the other four. For 1971, he swapped the BMW for an Alfa.

Two weeks after Schuster won at Loudon, Hans Ziereis raced his 2002 to victory at Bridgehampton. Ziereis had been a Porsche racer since 1959, but he switched to a 2002 in 1969, when his Foreign Cars of Hunterdon in New Jersey took on the BMW franchise. Along with his win at Bridgehampton, Ziereis also finished on the podium at Loudon and Watkins Glen in 1970, and he scored 2nd-, 3rd- and 4th-place finishes with his 2002 in 1971.

On the West Coast, Carl Fredericks Jr. was racing a 2002 under the banner of his father's Hyde Park Motors dealership in southwest Los Angeles. Fredericks Jr. had started racing a BMW 1800 in the Trans-Am series' West Coast rounds in 1967, then fielded a brand-new 1600-2 in 1968, most likely with a 2.0-liter engine.

Fredericks' #35 car was one of perhaps two delivered from Max Hoffman's truck and taken straight into the shop to be fitted with a roll cage and the other necessities of racing. Fredericks DNF'd his first race with the Hyde Park Motors car at Riverside, but he finished a promising 6th overall/1st in the Under 2-liter class at Kent that year. In 1969, he raced just one Trans-Am event, finishing 6th in class at Laguna Seca.

In late 1969, Hyde Park took delivery of a new 2002 and built it into a twin to Fredericks' racer. Driving the #34 Hyde Park car, new teammate Nels Miller opened the season credited with 2nd at Laguna Seca—until he was disqualified for oversize valves. (Fredericks was scored in 8th, having retired with 10 laps remaining.) At Kent, Miller finished 6th to Fredericks' 8th, and at Riverside Miller drove to 5th while Fredericks DNF'd.

Carl Fredericks races his Hyde Park Motors BMW in the Trans-Am series in 1968.

Except for a venture to Olathe, Kansas in 1971, the Hyde Park team would race mainly at Riverside through 1972, finishing no higher than 6th against ever-stiffer competition from Datsun and Alfa. In 1975, Fredericks entered the #34 and #35 2002s in the Riverside 6-hour race in 1975, driving the #35 to 20th with David Day. That was it for his Trans-Am career, and the Hyde Park 2002s were sold to Oceanside Motors, another SoCal BMW dealer. Mickey Pleasant raced the cars for Oceanside for years, then sold them to fellow dealer Rug Cunningham (Cunningham BMW in El Cajon), who did the same. Two of the original Hyde Park cars are vintage-raced to this day, owned by Steve Walker and Tim Brecht.

Also in California, Don Pike had been a race-winning Porsche driver before switching to a 2002 entered by Gregory Racing in 1970. Pike started the Trans-Am season with 2nd place at Laguna Seca, adding a 4th, a pair of 5ths and an 8th along with a trio of DNFs to complete the season. Those results were promising enough that Pike returned to the car for 1971, but this time he DNF'd five times while also finishing 2nd at Loudon, 5th at Road America and 6th at Riverside.

"The 2002 handled very well, especially on tracks like Laguna Seca, which I love," Pike said. "It was very easy to drive, and I really enjoyed it...except for the engines. One race it would have good horsepower, the next race it would hardly run. I knew you could buy a race engine from BMW, but the head mechanic wanted to build the engines himself, and something always went wrong. But it sure handled well."

Despite the 2002's excellent handling, the car remained at a disadvantage to the Alfas, and to Peter Brock's BRE Datsuns. Brock says the BMWs would have done better in Trans-Am if they'd gotten better support in dealing with SCCA rules that required nearly-stock engines and suspension.

"The European factories and engineers had zero experience building hot rods out of stock parts, and all their FIA-homologated racing equipment was illegal over here," Brock says. "The factories refused to engage. It wasn't that BRE had a huge budget, but we had better mechanics and fabricators, with the exception of the Wetson Alfa Romeo team."

Even if their results were less than stellar, the 2002 racers contributed greatly to BMW's visibility. Racing drew big crowds in the late '60s and early '70s, and the presence of competitive 2002s brought BMW to the attention of race fans nationwide.

In Europe, of course, the effect was far more dramatic. After dedicating its resources to F2 in 1967, BMW returned to the European Touring Car Championship in 1968. The ETCC's more liberal rules allowed BMW to enter a factory 2002 modified with suspension components from the works 2000 TI. That meant two-piece magnesium/aluminum wheels, a five-speed gearbox and limited slip differential, anti-roll bars, flared fenders, Plexiglas side and rear windows, and Kugelfischer fuel injection. Drivers Hubert Hahne and Dieter Quester had 205 hp at their disposal—not as much as the Porsche 911 or Alfa GTA, but enough to carry Quester to the 1968 ETCC title.

Hubert Hahne and Dieter Quester en route to victory at the Nürburgring in 1968.

Quester and the 2002 repeated as ETCC champs in 1969, the last year that BMW's factory team raced the 2002. For 1970, BMW switched to the E9 2800 CS, leaving the Type 114 to the private teams.

One of those teams, Alpina, had built 1600-2s and 2002s for BMW's factory rally team in 1967 and '68. Bovensiepen never really liked rallying, preferring the cleaner environment of road racing. In 1969, Alpina began racing in the ETCC with its own Type 114s, which Bovensiepen says marked a significant improvement over the New Class sedan.

"The 2002 was an affordable sports car, really. It had the proper dimensions for racing, much better than the [New Class]," Bovensiepen says. "It was an extremely important car for us, and extraordinarily successful in racing. It was this model which allowed us to demonstrate our pedigree and competence in touring car racing, and it was hence that Gert Hack and myself were able to kick-off and support the development of the CSL at BMW."

A true homologation special created by Alpina for BMW, the 3.0 CSL went on to countless wins for Alpina, BMW Motorsport, and other teams that had cut their teeth with the Type 114.

One was the team run by brothers Josef and Herbert Schnitzer, later by their half-brother Charly Lamm. Racing the 1600-2 and 2002, the Schnitzer team forged a close relationship with the BMW factory that continues to this day. From 1968, 2002s bearing the Schnitzer name appeared in the ETCC. The company also supplied complete racing engines to the BMW works team as well as privateers throughout the 2002's long production run.

Like the BMW factory team, Alpina and Schnitzer turned their attention to the E9 coupes from 1970, though Schnitzer later resumed its 2002 effort with a wild Group 5 car that featured a turbocharged engine and advanced aerodynamics. Throughout the 1970s, European companies like GS-Tuning, Hartge, and Faltz raced the 2002 with enthusiasm, the Heidegger Racing entry even winning the Group 2 Touring Class in the 1975 Le Mans 24 Hour.

The Schnitzer 2002s race for the first time at the Norisring in 1968.

Baur builds a cabrio

The Type 114 was intended from the start to be available in a variety of body styles, just like its predecessor the 700. "The general mentality was that we should do more with the 114 than just the two-door sedan," says David Carp, the longtime BMW Group designer who created and maintains the BMW Design Archive in Garching, near Munich.

The 700 cabriolet had been modestly successful—BMW sold 2,597 examples from 1962 to 1964—and a Type 114 cabriolet held at least similar promise.

BMW's Wilhelm Hofmeister-led design department began working on a convertible Type 114 in 1965. As *The cult car* reports, Hofmeister envisioned a "students' car," one that would be driven by the enthusiastic sons of wealthy parents. The car was sketched in-house as a 2+2 with a shorter rear overhang, a sloping tail, and a more steeply raked windshield than the standard Type 114 two-door.

BMW may have been designing its own convertible, but the company had never manufactured one. During the 1930s, it had relied on coachbuilders Wendler, Weinberger, Reutter, Gläser, Drauz, Baur, and Autenrieth to craft convertible bodies atop BMW chassis. When BMW began building cars again in 1952, only Baur of Stuttgart and Autenrieth of Darmstadt carried on the practice in any real volume. Both coachbuilders produced two- and four-door convertible versions of the 501 and 502 "Baroque Angels," which were offered through BMW dealers in Germany.

For its higher-volume 700 Cabriolet, BMW turned to Baur exclusively. When the Type 114 two-door replaced the 700 in 1966, Baur announced that its own coupe and cabriolet variants would follow; to retain control over the process, BMW formally commissioned Baur to create the prototypes.

At the same time, BMW asked Osnabrück coachbuilder Karmann—already producing the 2000 CS—to offer its own cabriolet prototype for consideration. Karmann designed a car that could seat two, not four, and that would require many new parts, both factors in its rejection.

Along with the German coachbuilders, BMW engaged the French firm of Brissonneau & Lotz to design additional body styles atop the Type 114. An engineering company involved in low-volume automobile production, B&L agreed in June 1966 to build cabriolet and roadster prototypes of the Type 114, and to show both at the Frankfurt auto show in September 1967.

BMW must have liked the idea of a roadster, because in October 1966 the board discussed building one with 1.6- and 2.0-liter engines. By the following summer, however, the board decided that the B&L concept was "unacceptable." We don't know which concept provoked that response, but the early B&L sketches in the BMW Design Archive reveal a wide variety of possibilities, many of which are simply impossible to imagine as a BMW.

Baur didn't bother with elaborate redesigns, opting to build a prototype of the "students' car" designed at BMW. Baur also created its own coupe, distinct from the Type 114 two-door, that featured a roofline borrowed from the 700 and equipped with "a draft-free sunroof" designed by Karl Baur.

When Baur presented its pair of prototypes, BMW sales chief Paul Hahnemann is said to have looked at both for about ten minutes before pointing to the cabriolet. "Baur, we'll take this one. You can keep the coupe."

In truth, the decision wasn't quite so simple. The "students' car" would have required too many expensive bodywork alterations, just like the Karmann concept, so Baur was asked to make another prototype that would be simpler

At Brissonneau & Lotz in 1967, Paul Bracq sketched a coupe and a roadster variant of the Type 114.

and cheaper to build.

Baur's second prototype was designed and engineered by Hermann Wenzelburger, who'd joined Baur in 1953 and worked on the earlier 501/502 and 700 convertibles. Wenzelburger removed the 1600-2's roof but left the sheet metal virtually unchanged below, at least so far as one could see. Without its roof, the Type 114 chassis lost considerable rigidity, so Wenzelburger reinforced the body shell around the A-pillar, side sills, and rear quarter panels.

Wenzelburger also gave the convertible a more steeply raked windshield, which resulted in a two-inch lower roofline. To ensure adequate headroom, the car got narrower, thinner front seats mounted closer to the floor. The rear seating area became smaller to accommodate the folding convertible top, and the radio antenna was moved to the decklid.

While Wenzelburger was designing his prototype, work on alternative roadster and coupe variants for the Type 114 continued at Brissonneau & Lotz.

In 1967, designer Paul Bracq had joined B&L from Mercedes, returning to his native France after 13 years in Stuttgart. Born in Bordeaux in 1933, Bracq was already a superstar in the design world. He'd begun his career working for French coachbuilder Philippe Charbonneaux in 1953 and '54; drafted into the French army, he ended up being stationed next door to Mercedes-Benz headquarters. After showing Mercedes his work, he was hired by the German automaker before his service had concluded.

Heading the Mercedes-Benz design studio, Bracq penned the highly regarded W113 roadsters and pagoda-roof coupes, as well as the stately W114/W115 coupes and sedans. At Brissonneau & Lotz, Bracq collaborated on the design for France's high-speed TGV trains, which are still in use today, and he also created new designs for a BMW 1600 TI coupe and convertible.

The coupe, Bracq says, was approved for production. Since BMW lacked the capacity to build it in Munich, Brissonneau & Lotz was contracted to do so itself à la Baur or Karmann.

"BMW was very happy with this car; unfortunately the French [carmakers] Peugeot and Renault forbade Brissonneau to built a German car in France," Bracq says. "I was very disappointed by this stupid, arrogant decision."

In the meantime, production of the Baur 1600 *Vollcabriolet* ("full cabriolet")—designated as the Type 114C within BMW—began in late 1967. The cars were assembled from complete knock-down (CKD) kits of parts shipped from Munich to Stuttgart, and the first examples reached the public in January 1968. Priced at DM 11,979 ($3,002), the drop-top carried a 38% premium over the standard 1600-2 two-door. The total could become even higher if the customer ordered real leather upholstery in place of the standard vinyl, custom paint, a zippered rear window, or any number of special

Designer Paul Bracq in 1971.

requests that Baur was ready to accommodate.

Despite the high price, BMW sold 1,682 (possibly 1,692) examples before the 1600 cabrio was superseded by the 2002 *Vollcabriolet* (E10/C, in accordance with the new *Entwicklung* designation) in January 1971.

Unfortunately, the more powerful engine highlighted the structural weakness of the cabriolet body, which suffered from excessive cowl shake and could even eject its windshield from the frame under hard cornering. What's more, convertibles were seen increasingly as dangerous anachronisms.

Safety regulations kept both *Vollcabrios* from being offered in the US, where testing had shown their windshield frames to offer insufficient rollover protection for the occupants in case of a crash. By the dawn of the 1970s, proposed safety regulations in Germany were threatening to kill the body style altogether, along with Baur's business. The firm needed a car that would let motorists enjoy top-down driving with fewer compromises to safety and handling.

Porsche had been offering its 911 Targa since 1967, and Wenzelburger was certainly aware of that car when he crafted his own Targa-style solution in early 1971. Since the Targa name was registered to Porsche, Wenzelburger called his car a "Cabriolet with Roll-bar." This new 2002 convertible had reinforced windshield pillars as well as a roll-over structure behind the driver's seat; a pair of beams joined the two together. A removable hardtop between windshield and roll bar was followed by a fabric soft-top, allowing configurations from fully enclosed to fully open. When not in place, the hardtop could be secured on brackets in the trunk.

The Baur-built 2002 Cabriolet with Roll Bar designed by Hermann Wenzelburger, shown here with its hardtop removed and its soft top folded down.

In May 1971, Wenzelburger and Karl Baur drove the bright yellow prototype from Stuttgart to Munich and parked it in front of the BMW administration building. Several board members, including Hahnemann, came outside to check it out. Decisive as always, Hahnemann reportedly walked around it once, put his hand on Karl Baur's shoulder and said, "Baur, we'll buy it."

Still designated E10/C, the 2002 Cabriolet with Roll-bar went into production in July 1971, hand-built in Stuttgart using some 3,000 parts from Munich. The car was priced at DM 14,985 ($4,306), again a 38% jump from the fixed-roof 2002 and an increase of DM 777 over the outgoing 2002 *Vollcabriolet*. The added safety and improved handling were worth the premium, certainly, to the 2,317 customers who purchased one. All were special-order cars available through the BMW dealer network, though not in the US. As with the *Vollcabrio*, the cars could be ordered with leather or cloth upholstery, as specified by the customer, and they could even be ordered with right-hand drive. BMW reports that some 354 customers in Japan, Britain, and South Africa ordered a right-hand drive Cabriolet with Roll Bar before production ended in December 1975.

Baur went on to build convertible versions of BMW's E21, E30 and E36 3 Series. The firm designed the E30 convertible built in-house at BMW from 1986, which may have sounded the firm's death knell. By 1998, Baur was insolvent, and its assets were taken over by prototype development firm IVM.

The 2002 Cabriolet with Roll Bar with its hardtop in place and its soft top attached to the roll bar.

TI and tii: More is never enough

Just as enthusiasts had wanted more performance than the original 1600-2 had to offer, eventually they wanted more than even the 2002 could provide.

Creating a hot-rod 2002 was easy, since BMW could follow the formula established by the 1600 TI. In fact, it was easier, because BMW already had a TI version of the 2.0-liter engine, introduced in the 2000 TI sedan in 1966. With two Solex 40 PHH carburetors and 9.3:1 compression, the 2.0-liter TI engine put out 120 (DIN) hp at 5,500 rpm and 125 lb-ft of torque at 3,600 rpm. That represented an improvement of 20 hp and 7 lb-ft over the standard 2002 engine, and of 15 hp and 26 lb-ft over the 1600 TI's twin-carb engine.

The 2002 TI was shown at Frankfurt in September 1968, just eight months after the 2002 had gone into production. Pitched not only at sporty driving enthusiasts but also at racers, the 2002 TI (**opposite**) rolled on track widths of 52.8 inches at both axles, 0.5-in. wider than those of a standard 2002. (All 1600s and 2002s had a 98.4-inch wheelbase.) The suspension arms were reinforced, as were the wheel hubs and bearings, and the front brake disc diameter increased from 240mm to 256mm. Wheels were half an inch wider, measuring 5.0 x 13 inches, mounted with 165HR-13 tires.

Inside, the 2002 TI came with a leather-wrapped steering wheel and a tachometer in the gauge cluster. From the outside, it was identical to the standard 2002 but for the "ti" badge on its trunk lid and grille.

With the standard four-speed manual gearbox, the 2002 TI could scoot from zero to 62 mph in 9.5 seconds; with the optional five-speed, 0-62 took only 9.1 seconds—nearly two seconds less than reaching the same benchmark in an ordinary 2002.

The 2002 TI served as the basis for BMW's factory rally cars, one of which took a class victory the Tour de Corse with driver Rauno Aaltonen in 1969. Aaltonen would rally that car in four events over 1970 and 1971, but he DNF'd with mechanical problems each time. In 1970, an Alpina 2002 TI won the German national rally championship with Helmut Bein and Hans-Christoph Mehmel, and in 1971 Poland's Sobieslaw Zasada drove a privately entered 2002 TI to a pair of victories (in Poland and East Germany) en route to the European Rally Championship. In 1972, Achim Warmbold and John Davenport drove the factory 2002 TI to BMW's first victory in the World Rally Championship, winning in Portugal.

By 1973, however, rallying was effectively over for both the 2002 and BMW Motorsport, which was concentrating solely on circuit racing with the CSL and its F2 engines.

Enthusiasts in the US were well aware of the 2002 TI's rally and racing activities. They'd rue its unavailability in the US just as they'd lamented the absence of the 1600 TI a year earlier, but neither of BMW's twin-carb cars could meet US emissions standards. Nor could BMW increase displacement, since the 2.0-liter M10 was already at its limit. Von Falkenhausen's team had tried enlarging it to 2.2 liters, as Dr. Karlheinz Lange noted in his seminal *BMW Engines*, but the larger engine "was found to have undesirable vibration properties while delivering no appreciable power increases."

To get more power while conforming to US emissions regulations, BMW would have to adopt fuel injection, a technology it had been discussing for that purpose since 1966.

Fuel injection had been developed in the 1920s for diesel engines, but it was also used on gasoline-burning radial aero engines during World War II, including BMW's 14-cylinder 801. The technology didn't make its way to

automobiles until the 1950s, and even then it was used primarily in racing thanks to superior operation at full throttle. As a result, fuel injection was associated with high performance, but its more precise fuel metering also meant lower emissions.

BMW came to fuel injection rather late. In 1967, the racing team used Lucas injection on its F2 engine, and a year later it adopted Kugelfischer mechanical fuel injection on its touring car racers.

Where the road cars were concerned, the BMW board of management first contemplated fuel injection at its meeting of January 18-19, 1966. Discussing the need to meet pending US emissions standards, board members agreed that fuel injection yielded better results. The expense of developing a fuel-injected motor for road cars dissuaded the board from approving the measure immediately; indeed, BMW waited until 1969 to create the fuel injected 2000 tii sedan. A fuel injected 2002 tii wouldn't become available until 1971, when tightening US emissions standards effectively forced BMW's hand.

The US already had the world's strictest emissions regulations when the 1970 passage of the Clean Air Act—along with President Richard Nixon's establishment of the Environmental Protection Agency—made them even stricter. From 1972-on, all new cars sold in the US would be subject to emissions testing, and they'd also need more smog-arresting equipment than the air pumps and EGR valves they'd had since 1968.

To satisfy US enthusiasts looking for more than the single-carb 2002's 113 SAE horsepower, BMW would need to install the fuel-injected 2000 tii engine from the New Class sedan. In place of Solex carburetors, the tii engine was equipped with Kugelfischer mechanical fuel injection, which used a three-dimensional cam to adjust the air-fuel mixture according to engine load, engine speed, and ambient temperature. It delivered 130 hp, marking a significant upgrade

over the twin-carb engine while delivering identical fuel economy. More important to enthusiast drivers, throttle response was much improved, with instant power and none of the "gulping" experienced with carburetors if the throttle was opened too quickly.

In Europe, the 2.0-liter fuel injected engine was available in the two-door 2002 tii from April 1971. Four months later, in August 1971, the US-spec 2002 tii went into production, offered as a 1972 model. Its 140-hp (SAE gross, later revised to 130 hp SAE net) made the 2002 tii a genuinely thrilling prospect in an age when substantial performance improvements were hard to come by.

Where the 2002 took 11.3 seconds to hit 60 mph, the 2002 tii needed just 9.8 seconds. The tii also had a higher top speed: 118 mph (as claimed by BMW) instead of 106 mph, which accorded with its preference for higher engine speeds.

"As with most such injected engines, the timed delivery of fuel to the ports makes it possible to use more radical valve timing and ram-tuned intake pipes without sacrificing low-speed tractability, and BMW does exactly that to extract the extra horses," noted *Road & Track* in October 1971.

"The tii's power peak is moved up to 5,800 rpm (the 2002 peaks at 5,500), but more significantly the torque peak of the injection engine occurs between 4,000 and 4,700 rpm compared to a mere 3,000 for the 2002. That torque peak is also much higher—145 lb-ft vs. the 2002's 116—but it is clear that the engine needs to be wound up to get the benefit of it."

The tii's chassis was up to the challenge of its engine. In England, *Autosport*'s John Bolster reported that the bodyshell had been reinforced to give greater rigidity. That allowed the tii to make the most of the upgraded equipment borrowed from the sportier 2002

TI: boxed rear semi-trailing arms, bigger front brakes (256mm discs rather than 240mm) with the same 230mm rear drums, a larger brake booster, half-inch wider wheels—"still not very wide at 5.0 in.," as *Road & Track* complained—and the option of H-rated Michelin XAS tires.

"In other words," said *Road & Track*, "the chassis has what it needs to handle the additional power; in Germany it has to be that way because people drive their cars as fast as they will go."

Here as well, the 2002 tii was exactly what performance enthusiasts wanted. From August 1971 through December 1974, BMW built 7,449 examples of the 2002 tii for export to the US. That total fell far short of the 77,638 standard 2002s (plus 14,271 2002 Automatics) exported from February 1968 to July 1976, but it was impressive nonetheless given the shorter production run and $4,000 price, about $1,000 more than the standard 2002.

The tii was certainly worth the premium, as *Road & Track* concluded: "The BMW 2002 tii is a keen sports sedan—a real blast to drive fast and yet practical enough for a small family to use for daily transportation and extended trips. The price is high and getting higher, thanks to the German currency's upward spiral, but the 2002 tii is bound to give BMW's little 2-doors a popularity boost. It certainly gave our collective mood a boost—it's nice to know that even with tightening smog regulations it's possible to get more performance in a car that was already strong in that department."

The strength of the car's performance featured prominently in new advertising created by the Harvey agency for Hoffman Motors. Still witty and wordy, the ads featured bolder type in keeping with the evolving design preferences of the early 1970s. As they had for the 1600-2 and 2002, the ads highlighted the tii's top speed—now a claimed 115 mph—as well as its exciting handling, mentioning only later that the car was roomy and practical, too.

Placed in magazines like *Road & Track* and *Car and Driver*, the ads complemented the favorable reviews of the new 2002 tii, helping to establish BMW as a serious contender for the hearts and wallets of US driving enthusiasts.

The Touring experiment

While the 2002 tii targeted performance enthusiasts, another Type 114 was aimed at drivers whose needs were more utilitarian. As BMW's press materials described the new hatchback at its 1971 launch, "The BMW touring models extend the BMW range with an attractive variant, of appeal both to the sportsman, who wants vitality, dynamism and long-distance comfort—and to the family father, who will also welcome the space and comfort on longer journeys."

The car was the 2000 tii Touring, presented at the Brussels Autosalon in January 1971. How this new body style came to be created has been something of a mystery, not least because BMW misreported the model's development process in *The cult car*. That book presents a detailed account of the 2002's development, but the 20+ years since its publication have seen new documents have come to light that refute several of its conclusions as well as its timeline.

We'll examine them here in chronological order.

As *The cult car* acknowledges, BMW's in-house design department had been working on a small sedan/wagon combination well before the takeover of Glas in 1966. But where the book says that such work began in 1965, board meeting minutes in the BMW Archive reveal that sales chief Paul Hahnemann suggested as early as November 1963 that the Type 114 range could be expanded beyond the two-door to include an estate car or wagon. Even before that board meeting, BMW's designers had sketched a car that looks very much like the 2002 touring. The sketches are preserved in the BMW Design Archive, and the dates of those documents helped founder David Carp determine the origins of the Touring body style.

The earliest Touring-related document (reproduced on p. 80) is dated April 25, 1963 and bears Georg Bertram's distinctive initial

"B." In this sketch, Bertram outlined a car with a touring-like profile and rear seat backs that fold forward to increase cargo space.

Bertram's drawing includes the car's dimensions, which reflect its origins as the successor to the 700 coupe. The car is specified at just 153.5 inches long overall, 53.5 inches tall, riding on a 96.0-inch wheelbase. (Eight years later, the production Touring would be 14 inches longer and two inches taller, riding on a 98.4-inch wheelbase.)

In March 1965, as the design for the Type 114 two-door was getting closer to reality—Bertram's final sketch for the 1600-2 is dated May 4, 1965—Bertram and fellow designer Manfred Rennen continued to sketch new versions of the hatchback.

"They're all very similar," Carp says. "They weren't competing; they were collaborating."

In 1965, the hatchback body style gets its own development designation. It's now known within BMW as the Type 114K, for "Kombi," though the car itself is called the "City." Bertram makes more drawings from September through December 1965; after that, the project goes dormant until Rennen picks up the thread in 1967.

We'll return to that in a moment, but first let's look at the 1004/1304 built by Hans Glas GmbH in nearby Dingolfing, which The cult car says might have influenced the Touring. As author Walter Zeicher writes, it was "a stylistically misconceived hybrid with a powerful engine—but hardly marketable." The "CL" version—for "Combi Limousine"—is a little better than the standard car, and this small station wagon is probably the specific model of 1304 to which Zeicher referred.

Interestingly, it appears to be the first car equipped with Glas' technically advanced four-cylinder engine, designed by Leonhard Ischinger with a belt-driven overhead camshaft. (Ischinger had designed the world's first all-aluminum V8 while still at BMW in the 1950s.) The car's steel monocoque body rode on trailing arm suspension up front, a rigid swing axle at the rear. It was reported to misbehave under both acceleration and braking, which must have been disturbing when combined with the 85-horsepower version of Ischinger's engine.

That engine was also used in Glas' 1300 GT, which debuted at the Frankfurt auto show in September 1963 and went into production in

Georg Bertram's sketch for the first BMW hatchback, dated April 25, 1963.

March 1964. The GT's stylish, well-proportioned bodywork was designed by Pietro Frua in Moncalieri, Italy (near Turin), crafted by the Maggiora coachworks near Frua's studio, and then shipped over the Alps for assembly at Glas. Powered by the aforementioned 1,290cc four-cylinder engine with 75 horsepower, the 1300 GT had a top speed of 106 mph. In September 1965, the 1300's output rose to 85 hp, and the car gained 3 mph in top speed. It also gained a 1700 GT counterpart that could hit 115 mph thanks to its 100-hp, 1,682cc engine. The latter was offered in the US as well as Europe, where its stylish bodywork and impressive performance drew positive reviews from enthusiast magazines.

Following BMW's 1966 acquisition of Glas, a few of the company's models remained in production, including the GT. The hatchback was modified to accept the BMW 1600's drivetrain and rear axle, and a double-kidney grille replaced the Glas logo. The BMW-Glas 1600 GT was introduced in June 1967, and it retired in May 1968. By then, more than 6,200 examples of the Frua-designed hatchback had been built, with Glas selling 5,000-plus units and BMW adding around 1,200 to the total.

At about the same time that BMW was installing the 1600's mechanicals into the Glas GT, Manfred Rennen was sketching new details for BMW's revived hatchback project.

A drawing by Rennen dated May 19, 1967 shows a rear view that incorporates the production 2002's round taillights, which are also seen in his more detailed drawings of June 2, 1967. At that point, the car still features six side windows, as it did in 1963; its C-pillar and

Equipped with a BMW drivetrain and a double-kidney grille, the BMW-Glas 1600 GT remained in production for a year after BMW's takeover of Hans Glas GmbH.

rear side windows are not yet finalized.

The drawings by Rennen and Bertram appear finished enough to serve as the basis for scale or even full-size models, but the BMW Board took a detour on June 15, 1967, pondering a pair of full-scale models from Italian designers Frua and Michelotti.

Frua had been invited to contribute to the design process for the Touring and other vehicles following BMW's acquisition of Glas, one of his largest clients. Michelotti had remained under contract with BMW since designing the 700 coupe, and he provided design sketches for various BMW concepts throughout the 1960s.

Carp notes that neither the Frua nor the Michelotti concept had much in common with the production Type 114 two-door, and they were very different from one another, as well. The Michelotti concept, he says, used rear surfacing that is very similar to that of the production Touring, and Carp believes that Manfred Rennen was asked to incorporate some Michelotti elements into his own design.

Rennen's sketch of June 2, 1967 demonstrates the Michelotti influence, as does the concept shown to the Board on August 18, 1967. By this point, Carp notes, the C-pillar has been finalized, complete with its two chrome strips and Hofmeister kink. The car is now called the "Break" rather than the "City," but in September that name is replaced by the new "touring" designation on the design drawings. By December, the name is set. (Presumably, the car has been designated E6 by this point, as well, the type designations having been retired in favor of E codes.) The board has signed off on the project, and no evidence exists that further exterior drawings were made after June 1967. A few drawings of badges were made along with those for accessories like a roof rack in September 1967, but otherwise the project was complete where exterior design was concerned.

The car sketched by Rennen had boxier, more upright proportions and less Ferrari-esque flair than the Glas GT. If the GT provided any inspiration, it wasn't in design but in proof of concept, perhaps convincing BMW of a hatchback's viability.

Even so, the Touring's development proceeded slowly even after the BMW-Glas GT went out of production in 1968. For reasons probably related to budget and/or production capacity, no interior sketches were made for the Touring until Wolfgang Seehaus—who'd come to BMW from Ford a few years earlier—applied his pen to the task in June 1969.

Shortly thereafter, in December 1969, Georg Bertram left BMW for Audi, and Paul Bracq took over leadership of the design department from Wilhelm Hofmeister.

By the time Bracq arrived, the Touring's design was finished. Bracq probably finalized some production-related elements, and he made a

An ad for the Glas 1700 GT appeared in *Road & Track*'s January 1967 issue.

series of drawings that were presented with the car at its launch. One shows a rear view of the car with its tailgate open, while others show the car from the side. "He was documenting, not creating," Carp says.

Bracq confirms Carp's assessment, insisting that he influenced only a few small details at the rear of the car upon his arrival at BMW. Bracq credits Michelotti for the design of the Touring, but the 1963-'67 sketches by Bertram and Rennen provide convincing evidence that the car was an in-house project from the start.

In its final production form, the car's front half was identical to that of Bertram's Type 114 two-door sedan. Its rear section was entirely new, the trunk replaced by a hatch that hinged at the trailing edge of the Touring's longer, lower (by 1.2 inch) roof, and with a profile suggested by Rennen's sketch of 1967.

Inside, the rear seat backs split, and they could be folded individually or together to add storage space in the cargo area, a feature meant to appeal to those carrying sporting goods or luggage for long trips. For the latter, the Touring also got a 6.0-liter larger fuel tank (to 52 liters) that gave it a generous 310-mile range.

All of those changes added up to a curb weight that increased by 110 lbs. compared to the two-door Type 114; with most of that weight up high and behind the rear axle, the Touring didn't handle quite as well as the standard 1600-2 or 2002.

The Touring's price was slightly higher, too, exceeding that of its comparable two-door counterpart by DM 700 ($201) when production

Manfred Rennen's sketch of June 2, 1967 shows the rear of the car then known as the "break" with the round taillights common to all early Type 114 production models.

began in April 1971. The Touring was offered as a 1600, 1800/1802, 2000/2002, 2000 Automatic, and 2002 tii, with the 2000 and 2002 available in right-hand drive.

Despite the proliferation of models, BMW built just 30,218 Tourings, far fewer than the company had hoped to deliver before production ended in April 1974.

Like the Baur-built convertibles, the Tourings were never exported to the US through official channels. The body style was rejected by then-importer Max Hoffman, who didn't think it would sell well in the US. Hoffman had a keen aesthetic sense, and he probably found the Touring inelegant. More practically, Hoffman didn't like stocking spare parts, and offering the Touring would have required considerable inventories of unique body panels and tailgate parts.

Despite underwhelming sales, the Touring exerted considerable influence as BMW prepared for the Type 114's replacement. Bracq used the Touring as a stylistic template for the first 3 Series, which he drew with an innovative hatchback that could be opened from the top or the middle.

As we'll see, Bracq's semi-Touring was never built, and BMW didn't make another hatchback or even a wagon until 1988, when the E6 Touring finally gained a successor in the E30 3 Series Touring.

Designers Wolfgang Seehaus (left) and Manfred Rennen (right) with an unidentified engineer at center. Sketches for the Type 114K/E6 Touring are pinned to the wall behind them.

The E6 Touring in its final production form, photographed in Munich in 1971.

The battery-powered Pacesetter

The pursuit of lower emissions—particularly in the US, where regulations were enacted toward that goal—had already led BMW to create the 2002 and the fuel-injected tii. In 1972, BMW would take it a step further, eliminating the internal combustion engine altogether in favor of electric power's zero-tailpipe emissions.

The project began in 1969, given the development code of E7 and conducted in utter secrecy. BMW's first battery-powered automobile began as an ordinary 1600-2 whose engine was replaced with twelve 12-volt batteries from VARTA, a Quandt Group subsidiary. While a purpose-built platform would have provided better distribution of the car's 2,929.3 lbs.—861.3 lbs. more than a standard 1600-2—the existing car had several advantages: It was cheap, it was readily available, and it allowed BMW to test a battery-powered car on the streets of Munich without attracting unwanted attention.

The batteries were connected in series, and mounted on a palette that allowed them to be removed and replaced as a unit. They could also be recharged without removal, connected to a power source via a socket behind the kidney grille, which opened to reveal it.

In addition to VARTA, BMW cooperated with Bosch, its principal supplier of electrical parts for series production cars. The Elektro Auto used a 43.5-hp Bosch DC motor, the output of which was controlled via a single "throttle" pedal in the driver's side footwell. A brake was present for emergencies, but otherwise the car was a true single-pedal car, its speed regulated by a Bosch pulse generator. It needed no gearbox, and its driveshaft connected directly to the rear differential via a reducing gear. Reverse was engaged via a small lever on the center console.

The Elektro Auto located the batteries in the engine bay and its motor where the transmission would normally be located. The control electronics were in the trunk, the fuse box and circuit breaker under the rear seat along with a supplemental 12-volt battery for the car's interior systems. Since the Elektro Auto had no radiator, the cockpit was heated electrically rather than by hot water, as were its front and rear windshields.

Instrumentation consisted of a speedometer that topped out at 120 km/h (75 mph), though the car could reach only about 90 km/h. A range indicator was included, providing a crucial point of data: At 50 km/h (31 mph), the Elektro 1600 could cover just 70 km, or 44 miles, before a recharge was needed.

After more than two years of development, the Elektro Auto was unveiled for the 1972 Munich Olympics. Two cars were made available to the organizers of the Games. They were used as stewards' vehicles for the marathon and speed-walking events, to which they were ideally suited thanks to their silent, emissions-free operation.

BMW showed off its green credentials with a poster advertising the Elektro Auto's role as "Schrittmacher," or pace-setter. Created by BMW's European ad agency, Gramm & Grey, the poster echoed the graphic style created by Otl Aicher for the Munich Olympics, and it featured the stars of the marathon running behind the zero-emissions Elektro BMW.

Although it had been created in anticipation of ever-more-stringent regulations in the US, the battery-powered car found new purpose with the OPEC oil crisis that hit Europe and the US two years later. Though the electric E7 was never offered to the public, BMW carried on with its alternative-power research. Most of the work centered on internal combustion engines that ran on natural gas or hydrogen as an alternative to gasoline, but the company continued to explore electric power.

In 2013, BMW launched its first series-production battery-electric car, the i3 "Megacity" that remains in the lineup along with gasoline-electric hybrids in every vehicle

Cutaway drawing shows the simplicity of the Elektro Auto's drivetrain.

category. It took more than four decades, but the i3 finally realized the potential demonstrated by the Elektro Auto at the 1972 Munich Olympics.

Even if electromobility merely shifts the pollution burden from the tailpipe to the power plant, electric vehicles have the advantage of silent operation, as the "Schrittmacher "demonstrated, and which BMW and the Olympic organizers recognized as a boon in itself, particularly in noisy, crowded cities.

Twelve 12-volt automotive batteries replaced the internal combustion M10 four in the Elektro Auto's "engine" bay. Note the shock tower modification required to accommodate the array.

Toward a Type 114 successor

When BMW's Type 114 two-door started coming off the line in March 1966, it was set to run through 1973, replaced by an all-new car for the 1974 model year. Instead, it remained in production through July 1977, receiving a mild but distinctive makeover while its successor was put on hold.

We'll look at the changes involved with that makeover in the next chapter. First, let's find out why the replacement was delayed.

The story begins with the arrival in Munich of Bob Lutz as BMW's new board member for sales in 1972. Lutz was 39 years old; along with 43-year-old chairman Eberhard von Kuenheim, he represented a new generation of leadership at BMW.

Lutz and von Kuenheim may have been contemporaries, but their experiences prior to joining BMW were vastly different. Von Kuenheim was born in 1928, a member of the landowning aristocracy in East Prussia. His father had died in an equestrian accident in 1935; ten years later, Eberhard fled his home as the Soviet army approached. His mother was captured by the Soviets and died in an NKVD camp.

Having reached West Germany, von Kuenheim worked in a Bosch factory making refrigerators and auto parts while earning a degree in engineering. Having specialized in automation technologies, he was hired by the Max Müller tool company and eventually became its technical director. In 1965, von Kuenheim joined the Quandt Group, advising Harald Quandt on technical issues.

After Harald's death in 1967, Herbert Quandt increased von Kuenheim's responsibilities within the Quandt Group. On January 1, 1970, Quandt appointed von Kuenheim chairman of the BMW board of management.

By contrast, Lutz had a international upbringing, away from the war that disrupted von Kuenheim's childhood. Born into a banking family in Lausanne, Switzerland in 1932, Lutz moved with his parents to Scarsdale, New York in 1939; in 1943, he became a US citizen. Four years later, Lutz returned to Switzerland to go to school.

After graduation, he joined the US Marine Corps as a fighter pilot, serving from 1954 to '59 and continuing to fly with the USMC reserves through the mid-'60s. He also attended the University of California at Berkeley, earning a bachelor's degree in production management in 1961 and an MBA in 1962. Lutz returned to Europe in 1963 and spent eight years at Adam Opel AG, the last three as board member for sales.

On January 1, 1972, Lutz joined a BMW board made up of von Kuenheim and longer-serving members Bernhard Osswald (R&D), Karl Monz (purchasing), and Hans Koch (production).

Replacing Paul Hahnemann as BMW's board member for sales, Lutz couldn't have been more different than his predecessor. Where Hahnemann was almost a broad-brush caricature of the glad-handing salesman, Lutz was a straight-arrow former Marine, a reputation that was reinforced by his background at GM. He was also known as a no-nonsense car guy, a real enthusiast with a strong understanding of BMW's brand identity.

"At my first meeting with my sales and marketing guys, they said, 'Mr. Lutz, you've got to get yourself over to Engineering—not Design—and look at the successor to the 1600 and 2002. It's so bad we don't want that car. We would rather continue with the 1600 and 2002 for a while, because that thing is a disaster.'"

After asking R&D chief Osswald to see the car, which he was told was finished, Lutz says he found the model in a tiny room, mocked up with real window glass, real trim and real tires. "It didn't look like a model until you looked through the glass and could see there was no interior," Lutz says.

Werner Hölbl's proposal for a 2002 successor, drawn in February 1970. The Viennese-born designer would go on to create the innovative Habicht SL binoculars for Swarovski.

The problem, Lutz says, was the car's body style. Despite underwhelming sales for the Touring, the 2002's successor had been configured similarly.

"It was a semi-hatchback, because they wanted to combine the Touring with the sedan, and only do one body style which would serve both markets," Lutz said. "That never works. So it was a hatchback that had a little trunklet added to it. And it was really bad."

Absent photos of the model seen by Lutz, it's impossible to confirm his impression of the car. We'll see Bracq's sketches on the following pages, but first let's look at how the car was created.

BMW had a design studio in 1972, but it constituted a division within body engineering, the department led by Wilhelm Hofmeister.

When Lutz arrived in 1972, the design studio leader was Paul Bracq, who'd replaced Georg Bertram when the latter left for Audi at the end of 1969. Then 39, Bracq came to Munich from Brissonneau & Lotz, where he'd designed the BMW roadster and coupe concepts we saw earlier. Prior to that, Bracq had led Mercedes' design studio, and returning to a manufacturer from a coachbuilder must have seemed at first glance like an occupational upgrade.

According to Lutz, Bracq's creativity was impeded by Hofmeister's conservatism and BMW's lack of resources for design.

"Paul Bracq was nominally chief designer, but he had no real studio, no employees, and he reported to Hofmeister, the former head of design," Lutz said. "Bracq was sort of crowded off into a corner, drawing a salary and completely frustrated. Hofmeister and the other Germans in body engineering didn't take him seriously. 'We don't need some BS Frenchman telling us how to design cars!'"

Design work for the first-generation (E21) 3 Series was well underway by the time Bracq arrived at the end of 1969, and so was work on the E12 5 Series, the successor to the New Class sedan. The two projects overlapped, since BMW wanted a coherent styling theme that would work across multiple platforms and on cars of various sizes. As a result, the 3 and 5 Series, in particular, have much in common where both inspiration and execution are concerned.

The earliest known sketch for a Type 114 successor (**page 90**) was drafted by Manfred

Marcelo Gandini's 1970 Garmisch prototype, as recreated by BMW Design in 2019.

Rennen on June 12, 1969. Rennen's car retains the Type 114's character line, though it does away with the chrome strip that defined this element on the 1600-2 and 2002. It features an interesting revision to the nose profile in which the hood extends past the grille, and its tail has been tucked under the trunk lid. Rectangular taillights replace the 2002's roundies, offering better illumination as well as an updated look.

While Rennen was sketching in Munich, BMW was soliciting additional proposals from outside firms, as it had done throughout the 1960s.

In February 1970, Viennese designer Werner Hölbl—whose studio was then in Turin, Italy—offered a pair of sporty interpretations with four round headlights instead of two, and rectangular taillights. Neither of these really moved the goalposts, though they did propose a new view of the car's front and rear within the existing profile.

Another designer in Turin, Bertone's Marcello Gandini, created not just sketches but a prototype. Called the Garmisch, this fully-developed concept was shown at Geneva in March 1970. Recently recreated by BMW Design to acknowledge Gandini's role in the creation of the E12 5 Series, the Garmisch influenced Bracq's sketches of May 10, 1970 (**opposite**).

Like the Garmisch, Bracq's Type 114 successor was a sharper-edged, more angular vehicle than anything BMW had produced to that point. It also featured Bracq's innovative, double-hinged rear portal, which could open from the middle like a trunk or from the top, as a hatchback.

As mentioned above, we don't know what the actual prototype looked like as seen by Lutz in 1972, but the car sketched by Bracq in 1970 is far from unattractive, as Bracq himself is right to point out.

"My first idea was to design the new 3 Series with a rear door à la Touring, but Lutz told me that German customers, mainly, prefer a classic sedan look," Bracq says. "It was not an ugly car, and it was a success when I presented it to Mr. Quandt, the most important person at BMW."

The front can't be seen in the drawings, but Lutz says it abandoned BMW's trademark kidney grille in favor of horizontal bars across the front. "I said that's out of the question, because BMW has this rich front-end identity that nobody else has, consistent over the decades, which is the two kidneys."

It's hard to imagine Bracq himself abandoning that design element, having used it to good effect in all of his earlier BMW concepts at Brissonneau & Lotz. Regardless, Lutz says that BMW board chairman Eberhard von Kuenheim didn't like the proposed car, either. Both men convinced the rest of the board to put the Type 114's replacement on hold until the car could be redesigned. In the meantime, the car would receive new design details and functional upgrades.

(Opposite) As sketched by Paul Bracq in 1970, the successor to the Type 114 featured an innovative trunk/hatchback combination that could be opened from the top or the middle. The car advanced to the prototype stage, but it never reached series production.

Square taillights and big bumpers

In its ninth year on the market, beginning with September 1973 production, the 2002 was given its first significant updates. As the E10/73, it received larger and brighter rectangular taillights that were distinctly more modern-looking than the small "roundies" of the original design, and which echoed the taillights on the E12 5 Series that debuted in 1972. All of the Type 114/E10 models received the new taillights save the Touring, whose unique body panels and low sales volume decreed retention of the round taillights. Elsewhere on the exterior, the E10/73 received a low-gloss black radiator grille with larger kidneys, still in chrome, and a BMW roundel on the previously unadorned trunk lid.

Inside, the instrument panel was redesigned with simulated wood veneer in the gauge surround. The interior also got a four-spoke padded steering wheel, better front seats, headrests and seat belts as standard equipment, one-piece door panels, and revised control stalks on the steering column.

Mechanical changes for the 1602 (as the 1600-2 had been renamed for 1971), 1802, and 2002 included wider wheels, a larger fuel tank, larger brake booster, better muffler, and smaller clutch; the 2002s also got halogen headlights, and the Automatic got a new Solex 32/32 DIDTA carburetor.

In the US, the smaller-engined car had exited the lineup following the 1971 model year, but the 2002 received all of the styling updates noted above. Federal regulations required retention of less-effective sealed beam headlights, however, and mandated additional safety equipment like the 5-mph "diving board" bumpers that protruded from the car's body by several inches. The big bumpers detracted significantly from the 2002's attractive profile, and they also added unwanted weight well beyond both axles. They weren't well received by enthusiasts, who preferred the more elegant look and lighter weight of the smaller but admittedly less effective bumpers on the earlier cars.

Production of the fuel-injected 2002 tii was discontinued for the US in December 1974, though it continued through June of 1975 for other markets, and through October 1975 for right-hand drive models. That's when production of the carbureted 2002 ended for all markets but the US, for which 2002s continued to be produced through July 1976. The final cars received a revised cylinder head, exhaust system, and seats, plus additional emissions control equipment like a larger EGR valve required to keep the 2002 compliant fully eight years after it had first arrived in the US.

1975 US sales brochure for the 2002 and 2002 tii shows the car with its "diving board" bumpers, designed to meet new 5-mph impact standards.

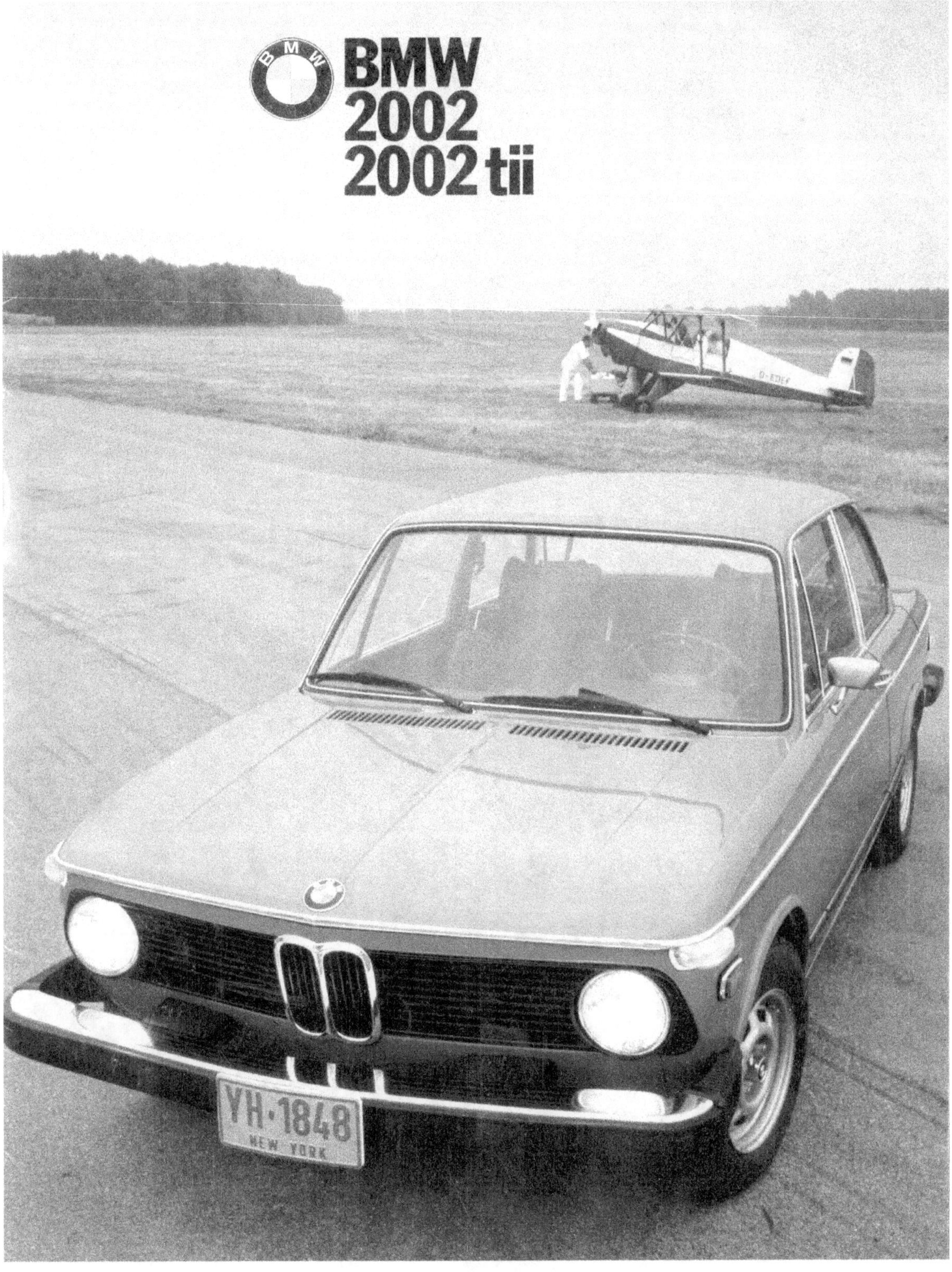
BMW
2002
2002 tii
YH·1848
NEW YORK

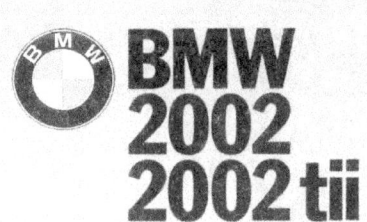

Edition L

Edition L, for Luxury

Following its September 1973 facelift, BMW's 1602 and 2002 got a new option package to sustain sales and interest. A Bob Lutz project, the "Edition L" variant was offered from April 1974, and it brought unprecedented luxury to BMW's small two-door.

Identifiable on its exterior only by a stylized "L" under the 2002 badge on the rear panel, the "Luxury" model was noteworthy for its interior appointments. It had the updated four-spoke steering wheel, deep velour carpeting, and door panels with storage pockets and genuine wood veneer trim, which was echoed on the dashboard at Lutz' insistence.

"That was another, 'Oh my God, we don't do that at BMW!' Why not? 'Well, wood is old-fashioned, it's Mercedes, and our owners don't like it.'" Lutz said. "I said, 'Well, how about just a little walnut in the instrument cluster?'

"That was part of the freshening to give it another couple years of life until we could bring out the 3 Series."

With the "L" model, Lutz got his walnut on the dash, and a solid wood shift knob to go with it. The "L" model also got more supportive seats with upgraded vinyl upholstery that carried over onto the rear parcel shelf. The rear bench seat got a center armrest, and the front seats were equipped with automatic three-point seat belts. A rear-window defroster was standard, along with intermittent windshield wiper operation, a carpeted trunk, and a lockable gas cap. Radios, alloy wheels, and heat-resistant window glass were available as extra-cost options.

The "L" package was priced at DM 720 ($279) in Germany, and it was offered through the end of production on all Type 114/E10 hardtop models except the 2002 turbo. Exactly how many cars were optioned with the "L" package is unknown—the number is said to be 1,200, all for the European market—but BMW says it "found widespread appeal among customers."

Turbo power for the '02

Given that US enthusiasts had already been denied the twin-carburetor 1600 and 2002 TI, the convertibles, Tourings, and even the Luxury Edition, they probably weren't surprised when BMW introduced the 2002 turbo in January 1974 with no plans to bring it to the US. With a 170-horsepower turbocharged 2.0-liter engine and racing-inspired bodywork, it represented the ultimate expression of 2002 performance, and it put the long-running model back on the cutting edge of automotive technology.

The 2002 turbo was conceived by Bob Lutz, who was keen to protect and expand BMW's reputation as a maker of driver-oriented automobiles and sporty long-distance motorcycles. One of his first moves upon arriving at BMW had been to create BMW Motorsport, the racing division that also developed and promoted high-performance automobiles like the 3.0 CSL Batmobile.

The CSL served BMW well at the high end of the sporty market, but Lutz felt the company needed something equally compelling in the compact segment. "Ford was starting to develop some very fast Capris, and GM wasn't sitting on its hindquarters," Lutz said. "[BMW's] market appeal was always more handling, better brakes, and more performance, and that was at risk. It was important for us to do a car that was head and shoulders above anybody else's, in a compact format."

To create it, Lutz turned to BMW Motorsport. The factory team had raced and rallied the Type 114 prior to the arrival of the E9 coupe in 1968, and then alongside the larger car through 1972. Alpina and Schnitzer raced (and rallied) the 1600 and 2002 with considerable success, too, both teams working closely with the factory to develop the car's potential.

The M10 engine had proved well suited to racing modifications, and by 1968 the BMW factory and Schnitzer had developed a naturally aspirated 2.0-liter version that produced around 200 hp. Even so, the racing 2002s were still down on power to the 220-hp Alfa Romeo GTA-SAs and 230-hp Porsche 911s (which were also much lighter) against which they raced in the European Touring Car Championship.

The horsepower deficit didn't stop BMW factory driver Dieter Quester from winning the title that year, but BMW engine chief and racing boss Alexander von Falkenhausen knew he'd need more firepower in 1969. Von Falkenhausen was no fan of forced induction, but he directed his team to turbocharge the engine nonetheless. "We won't be able to beat the Porsches in the European Touring Car Championship otherwise."

Von Falkenhausen assigned the task to 34-year-old Paul Rosche, the Munich native who'd joined BMW straight out of the city's technical university—just like von Falkenhausen a generation earlier. Rosche developed the turbocharged 2.0-liter four-cylinder to put out 275 hp at 6,500 rpm and 236 lb-ft of torque—so much power that the car required much wider tires behind flared fenders.

The turbocharged engine proved fragile, and Quester raced just as often with a naturally aspirated engine. Rosche called the engine "atrocious," and it's said to have emitted black clouds of exhaust smoke at its first race. It improved over the course of the season, of course, and turbocharging seemed likely to find wider use within BMW after Quester repeated as champion in 1969. "At the very first test runs of the turbo on the dyno, we were asking

(Left) Bob Lutz on a BMW R75/5 motorcycle in front of the BMW Museum. (Right) Alex von Falkenhausen and Paul Rosche on pit wall in 1967.

ourselves if this couldn't be something for F1," Rosche said. "The potential power seemed to be inexhaustible."

For 1970, however, the ETCC required all turbocharged cars to be fully homologated for Group 2, with no fewer than 1,000 street-legal examples built for the road. BMW had no plans to build a turbocharged 2002 road car, so it abandoned the project and left GT racing to the privateers, focusing the factory effort on the naturally aspirated M12 for Formula 2. That M10-based engine would itself be turbocharged a few years later; in the meantime, the turbocharged engine from the 1969 season was put to work providing motive power as well as a theme for BMW's first-ever concept car, the BMW Turbo.

This project, too, was a Lutz initiative. With the 1972 Olympics being staged literally across the street from BMW's Munich headquarters, Lutz saw an opportunity to garner valuable attention for the marque. Von Kuenheim had intended to mark the occasion by premiering the forthcoming E12 5 Series sedan, but Lutz convinced him that the company needed to make a bigger splash, to demonstrate BMW's technical prowess on a grander scale.

"If this were GM or Ford," Lutz told von Kuenheim, "what we would do is a special Olympics concept car, something really way out there that will blow people away."

BMW had never built a concept car, but Lutz knew exactly what was required. First, he needed a platform.

"Engineering had two old chassis prototypes, which were the BMW 2000 platform but with a transverse-mounted four-cylinder turbo engine," Lutz said. "They were toying with the idea of doing a mid-engine four-door sedan,

Paul Bracq with his Turbo concept of 1972.

which was a ridiculous proposition."

Lutz found an enthusiastic ally in Paul Bracq. Finally free to exercise his imagination, Bracq sketched a futuristic wedge-shaped body, which BMW dubbed the "Turbo" after its engine. The concept had the shape of a supercar, but it was designed for more than mere performance. Lutz had fleshed out the concept by borrowing a number of avant-garde safety features from Bill Mitchell at General Motors, like the deformable plastic nose and radar-utilizing brake zone detection. "We never put that in, because the technology wasn't ready, but there were little radar antennas up front and a screen inside," Lutz said.

The Turbo concept was a huge hit when it was shown at Paris in September 1972. It created a favorable buzz around the notion of turbocharging, even though that was only peripheral to the car's purpose. It also put turbocharging at the forefront when it was time to boost the 2002's performance beyond what even the tii could achieve.

Lutz was well aware of the racing team's 1969 experiments with the turbocharged 2002, and he figured that its engine could be adapted for use on a high-performance road car.

"They had a 2.0-liter turbo engine ready to go that nobody was really interested in using, and I said, 'Why don't we put that in with an intercooler and we'll do wheel arch extensions and we'll give it a wider track, we'll give it a deep front spoiler and so forth, so on.' That's what we did," Lutz said.

To create the E10/T, BMW Motorsport started with the 2002 tii's familiar 1,990cc M10 four with Kugelfischer fuel injection. Motorsport redesigned the cylinder head and installed new pistons for a lower compression ratio (6.9:1 rather than 10.0:1), then fitted a modified injector pump, and a Kühnle, Kopp, and Kausch (KKK) turbo adapted from a light truck application to produce 0.55 bar of pressure. Interestingly, the installation didn't include a blow-off valve: Reporting in *Road & Track*'s July 1974 issue, Paul Frére writes that one was tried but found to have a negligible effect on power or turbo lag.

Output rose from the tii's 130 hp to 170 hp at 5,800 rpm and from 133 lb-ft to 181 at 4,000 rpm, enough to make the relatively light (2,376-lb.) 2002 turbo complete the 0-to-62 mph dash in 6.9 seconds rather than the 9.4 needed by the tii. Top speed increased to 131 mph, 13 mph faster than the tii despite the additional frontal area created by the fender flares and spoilers designed by Bracq in the style of the 1969 factory race cars.

The turbocharged engine and its plumbing pack the 2002's engine bay. 2002 turbo interior featured sport seats, a three-spoke steering wheel, a boost pressure gauge, and a red instrument surround.

"In town the engine proved extremely smooth and tractable but slightly gutless in the lower speed ranges—not surprising in view of the low compression ratio and the comparatively high exhaust back pressure," Fréres wrote. "It was not before a short stretch of *Autobahn* was reached, on the way to BMW's test track, that the car showed its Jekyll-and-Hyde character by the way it rocketed up to the provisional 100-km/h (62-mph) limit. This speed, by the way, is reached in 2nd of the four gears in the standard gearbox."

The Porsche 911 Carrera was faster from zero to 62 and had a higher top speed, but that car cost twice as much as a 2002 turbo. Priced at DM 18,720 ($7,256), the BMW was the high-performance bargain of 1974.

For the price, 2002 turbo buyers also got a 20mm front anti-roll bar instead of the tii's 15mm bar, stiffer rear springs with adjustable ride height, and Bilstein dampers. The trailing arms were reinforced, as were the rear wheel bearings, hubs and stub axles. The front brakes were the same 10.08-inch diameter, but the turbo received vented instead of solid rotors, and larger 10.0-inch rear drums in place of the tii's 9.0-inch rear brakes. The wheels were still 13-inchers, but the 2002 turbo got 185-section width radials in place of the tii's 165s. It also got wider tracks: 54.1 inches front/53.6 inches rear, an increase of 1.27 and 0.77 inches, respectively, accommodated by the turbo's distinctive flared fenders.

The interior featured a dashboard with a gauge surround in red, plus deeply bolstered bucket seats and a leather-wrapped steering wheel. The turbo was available in just two colors: Chamonix white or Polaris silver, either of which could be decorated with tricolor Motorsport stripes that further distinguished

Created following the updates of September 1973, all 2002 turbos feature rectangular taillights. As Euro-only models, all were equipped with the smaller bumpers used in that market.

the E10/T from a run-of-the-mill 2002.

On the front spoiler, the graphics spelled out "2002 turbo" in reverse, to let other drivers identify the car in their rear view mirror. Bracq says the idea was Lutz's, inspired by the reverse lettering on Swiss ambulances.

Those graphics helped doom the 2002 turbo, which had been introduced at the worst possible time for a high-performance car, politically speaking. In response to increasing traffic fatalities, Germany had imposed its first speed limits, restricting drivers on back roads to 100 km/h (62 mph). That wasn't all. The turbo's debut coincided with the OPEC oil crisis, which further vilified fast cars. Newspaper editorials called for a ban, and the 2002 turbo was held up in Germany's *Bundestag* as an example of the auto industry's "irresponsible excesses."

BMW replaced the reverse "turbo" lettering with plain striping during the first month of production, but it wasn't enough. The 2002 turbo would be discontinued after only a short run. Following the 12 pre-production examples built between July and December 1973, a mere 1,660 production-spec 2002 turbos came off the line between January 1974 and July 1975. All were left-hand drive models sold from new in Europe; the car never came to the US as an official import, though quite a few were imported privately over the years.

The 2002 turbo was stripped of the reverse "turbo" lettering on its front spoiler about a month into its production run.

The cult car says the turbo was incapable of meeting US emissions requirements, but Frére's review in *Road & Track* suggested otherwise.

"In the exhaust-emissions department, the Turbo is better than its unsupercharged equivalents as far as NOx is concerned because of its low internal compression ratio, and is about the equivalent of the 2002 tii for HC and CO; the emission test program is such that the blower hardly comes into its own," Frére wrote.

"Wouldn't it be nice if BMW were planning this approach to meeting the tough 1975 American emission standards?" he concluded.

It was an interesting speculation, particularly in light of BMW's return to turbocharging in 2006. Today, virtually every BMW engine is turbocharged, which the company acknowledges is the only way to achieve high performance, fuel efficiency, and low emissions simultaneously.

Turbocharging had the same effect on the 2002 turbo. Although it came under fire during the OPEC oil crisis, the 170-hp 2002 turbo returned 22 mpg while cruising at 68 mph, significantly better than the 18 mpg returned by the 130-hp 2002 tii.

The turbo aroused controversy when new, and Lutz was made to account for its excesses. It may have been politically incorrect, but Lutz thinks BMW was right to build it. "I felt the 2002 turbo was protecting the brand image," he said. "The 2002 turbo was a lot of fun. Unfortunately, it got me into a lot of trouble."

Lutz takes on Hoffman

As board member for sales, Bob Lutz (**opposite, at right**) exerted considerable influence on BMW's product portfolio, spurring the creation of the 2002 turbo and the 2002 Luxury Edition while effecting the redesign of the E21 3 Series. He created BMW Motorsport, putting the company's racing activities on a structural footing that has lasted to this day.

Lutz's more profound and lasting achievement, however, involved not BMW's products but its export practices, which he transformed entirely in cooperation with board chairman Eberhard von Kuenheim (**opposite, at left**).

In the early 1960s, prior to Lutz's arrival, the New Class sedan had brought BMW to profitability for the first time in the postwar era, but that car's success was modest compared to what would follow with the Type 114, and it was largely contained to the German market.

While forecasting production of the Type 114, BMW had estimated that exports would account for at least one-third of sales. The 1600-2 and 2002 fulfilled that expectation handily. Worldwide demand became so great, in fact, that BMW purchased Hans Glas GmbH to gain a skilled workforce and expansion potential in Dingolfing. The company also moved motorcycle production to Berlin so that Munich's full capacity could be dedicated to small-car production. (BMW Werk 1 in Munich-Milbertshofen remains the center of 3 Series production worldwide.)

The Type 114 represented BMW's first global success, and nowhere was its impact more profound than in the US.

In 1966, the year prior to its debut, BMW had exported just 1,253 cars to the US. In 1967, exports to the US jumped to 4,564 cars, of which 4,362 were new 1600-2s. In February 1968, the 1600-2 was joined by the 2002, and BMW's US exports more than doubled by the end of the year, with exports reaching 9,172 cars, including 3,892 new 2002s.

With that, the US became BMW's biggest export market, and the brand appeared to be on an upward trajectory.

In 1969, BMW explored a cooperation with American Motors for assembly of 2002s for the US market, which would be sold through the AMC dealer network, but that notion was abandoned when Hahnemann found AMC incapable of building cars to the BMW standard. That year, BMW's US exports escalated to 6,962 of its 2002s, plus 2,675 affordable 1600-2s.

BMW had clearly expected more, and it was doubly disappointed in 1970, when US auto sales declined sharply overall and 2002 sales fell to 6,667 units before rising to 9,010 in 1971.

US customers had to wait several months before receiving their cars, suggesting unmet demand, but sales of the 2002 would hover around 9,000 units annually from 1971 through 1973. The E3 Bavarias and E9 coupes continued to attract new buyers, however, and BMW's exports to the US totaled 11,338 in 1969; 10,029 in 1970; 13,560 in 1971; 15,113 in 1972; and 13,789 in 1973.

Those figures meant that BMW remained last among foreign marques in the US, selling half as many cars as Mercedes and fewer than even the English branch of Ford.

The US market represented vast untapped potential for BMW—and not only where volume was concerned. By the early 1970s, BMW found itself in the same position as Mercedes in the late 1950s: exporting its cars to the US in ever-greater quantities, but losing money nonetheless.

Common to both scenarios? Max Hoffman, who imported Mercedes to the US until his contract was terminated in 1957, one year in advance of its expiration, and who became BMW's US importer in 1962.

It was BMW's second go-round with Hoffman. As we've already seen, BMW agreed to let Hoffman import the 507 and 503 in 1957, only to terminate that deal a year later when Hoffman reneged on purchase agreements, payments, and import volume.

Crucially, Hoffman wasn't BMW's sole importer at the time. He'd muscled in on the contract held by Fred Oppenheimer's Fadex company, which made it relatively easy for BMW to cut him loose when the 507 project went south.

Oppenheimer had considerable success with BMW's sub-1,000cc machines, selling more than 15,000 Isettas, 600s, and 700s between 1955 and 1961. He might have done well with the New Class sedans and Type 114s, too, but he never got the chance. The Fadex contract was expiring just as the New Class was ready for export, and BMW chose not to renew.

In March 1962, BMW awarded its US import contract to Max Hoffman, the same distributor who'd helped drive the company to near-bankruptcy just three years earlier.

Max Hoffman in 1963.

Which begs the question: Why?

It's impossible to review BMW's entire decision process, since minutes from board meetings held from 1960 into 1963 no longer exist in the BMW Archive. Nonetheless, enough documentation remains to allow meaningful interpretation of events. Even thought the account is one-sided, it's clear that Hoffman is no hero in this story.

As we saw in Chapter II, BMW's leadership was in flux following the shareholder's revolt of December 1959. Heinrich Richter-Brohm resigned as chairman in early 1960, and he wasn't replaced until the beginning of 1962, when new majority shareholder Herbert Quandt sent Karl-Heinz Sonne to BMW from the Quandt Group's Concordia electric company.

Sonne's appointment had been unpopular among BMW executives—Horst Mönnich reports that they considered Quandt "meddling," believing him to own just 10% of BMW stock rather than nearly half of the company—and it led to discord and departures.

One who left was Ernst Kämpfer, who'd held several board positions including sales from February 1958. He became the unofficial chairman when Richter-Brohm left, and he in turn departed when he was bypassed for the post in favor of Sonne.

Taking over Kämpfer's former sales position was Paul Hahnemann, who joined as a deputy board member in September 1961, just prior to Sonne's arrival. Unlike Sonne, he was a seasoned auto executive who'd spent his career with GM and Auto Union, making him the only BMW board member with international experience in the industry.

Given what followed, we can assume that the persuasive Hahnemann encouraged the initial re-engagement with Hoffman, and that Hoffman's strong capital position justified the decision to the other board members.

The initial contract with Hoffman of March 1962 required him to purchase 1,000 cars from 1962 to 1964, followed by 1,500 cars annually after that. It also required him to provide "powerful service"—meaning the spare parts, technical assistance to dealers, and after-sales service that had been lacking in Hoffman's representation of Mercedes and other marques. If none of that happened to BMW's satisfaction, the contract expired at the end of 1964.

Hoffman came close to meeting the volume target, importing 720 cars in 1962 and 231 in 1963. It's impossible to know whether he provided "powerful service," but it didn't matter. In 1963, Hoffman's contract was redrafted to extend through 1970—apparently at Hahnemann's instigation, since the board proposed making Hahnemann himself responsible for "all possible damages suffered by BMW AG under the Hoffman contract."

By then, Hahnemann had become a full member of the board, affording him even greater influence over BMW's business practices. His influence likely increased when Sonne departed unexpectedly at the end of March 1965, replaced a day later by Gerhard Wilcke. A Quandt Group lawyer who'd been serving on BMW's supervisory board, Wilcke lacked a background in engineering or the auto industry, which made him a relatively weak chief executive. Worse, perhaps, majority shareholder Herbert Quandt was becoming less involved with BMW's management, creating an opening for a strong personality like Hahnemann's to exert itself.

As for Hoffman, he had a powerful incentive to maintain his US distributorship of BMW: By 1965, it was the only marque he represented.

Though he'd introduced nearly two dozen European marques to this country since opening his New York dealership in 1949, he'd lost one after another starting with Volkswagen in 1953. Jaguar and Mercedes broke off with Hoffman in 1954 and '57, respectively, Fiat in 1958. In 1959, Porsche took away Hoffman's sole US rights, reducing him to one of seven regional distributors and then eliminating him altogether when it created its own sales subsidiary in 1964, just as Alfa Romeo had done three years earlier. When Lancia transferred its US distributorship to Luigi Chinetti in 1965, Hoffman was left with a single marque: BMW.

To get out of their contracts with Hoffman, most if not all of those automakers paid substantial sums—millions of dollars, plus a sizable fee on every car sold for the duration of the original contracts.

In telling his story to Karl Ludvigsen and other journalists, Hoffman claimed that he had "given up" the other marques to "focus" on BMW. On the contrary, every marque he'd represented had broken off with him, usually for his failure to provide adequate marketing and after-sales support for their automobiles, but also because manufacturers like Mercedes were losing money while Hoffman was getting rich. (Hoffman professed an indifference to money, but he had lavish homes in Beverly Hills, Palm Beach, Munich, and Rye, New York, the latter commissioned from Frank Lloyd Wright, who'd also designed the showroom at 430 Park Avenue that Hoffman lost to Mercedes in 1957.)

Such was the case at BMW, which saw losses of DM 2.7 million ($675,000) on its 1966 US exports.

Even though the board had threatened to hold Hahnemann responsible for any damages incurred following the 1963 extension of the Hoffman contract, he apparently suffered no repercussions. On the contrary, Hahnemann signed yet another contract with Hoffman in 1967, this time cementing Hoffman's sole distributorship rights for the US.

Hahnemann had come to consider himself "co-CEO" with Wilcke, and he couldn't have been pleased when he was passed over for the chairmanship when Wilcke resigned for health reasons at the end of 1969. (Earlier that year, he'd told *Der Spiegel* he "preferred to remain a salesman," which the magazine noted

The Harvey agency continued to create clever ads for BMW through the 1970s, but Hoffman placed them only sporadically in magazines like *Car and Driver* and *Road & Track*.

brought a DM 400,000 annual salary that likely exceeded Wilcke's.) Instead of Hahnemann, Wilcke was replaced by yet another Quandt Group executive: 40-year-old Eberhard von Kuenheim.

Hahnemann subjected von Kuenheim to public ridicule, calling him "BMW's most expensive apprentice." Von Kuenheim kept his cool, but he started looking for malfeasance and found plenty, according to Bob Lutz.

"Von Kuenheim found out that Hahnemann was passing all of BMW's catalog and print materials business—at vastly inflated prices, by the way—to a printing company owned by his mistress, in collusion with the advertising agency," Lutz said. "We figured that Hahnemann had stolen about $10 million."

Von Kuenheim forced Hahnemann from the board on October 28, 1971, but the corruption he'd engendered went deeper than just printing contracts. Far more problematic were the contracts he'd signed with BMW's foreign distributors, which Lutz began examining when he replaced Hahnemann as BMW's board member for sales at the beginning of 1972. "I showed von Kuenheim the profit and loss statements of the six largest European distributors, and their profit on 35,000 cars was higher than BMW AG's from selling 200,000 cars."

The situation was equally unfavorable in the US, where BMWs were distributed by Hoffman Motors Corporation.

"Maxie was not a good distributor," Lutz told *Bimmer* magazine. "He was a colorful personality, but his ethics were more than questionable."

In 1971, with the 2002 in its fourth year of production, BMW projected US sales opportunities of 40–50,000 cars per year; Hoffman sold 13,560.

To make matters worse, Hoffman was making around $1,000 in profit per car while BMW earned a few hundred, when it made money at all from its US exports. Each E3 Bavaria, a bare-bones model created at Hoffman's insistence, sold at a loss to BMW, which considered its sub-$5,000 price "dumping." The losses convinced BMW in November 1972 to stop selling its large cars in the US after 1977. (That decision was later reversed, and the first-generation 7 Series arrived in the US for the 1978 model year.)

The financial situation tilted in Hoffman's favor on the retail level, too. Even though BMW's retail prices were the highest in their class, dealers earned lower margins (14.2%) on BMWs than they did on comparable marques (16% on VW, 20% on Fiat). Dealers weren't happy with the parts supply or the technical assistance they received from Hoffman Motors, either. Nor did they think he was marketing the brand sufficiently.

"I didn't think he was advertising enough," says Lee Maas, who began selling BMWs from his Classic Cars, Inc. dealership near Dallas in 1971. "I wrote him a letter and told him rather matter-of-factly that he should be doing a better job. Later, I went to see his new warehouse in New Jersey, visit the staff, and as I was leaving they said, 'Mr. Hoffman wants to see you.' He was sitting in his chair, leaning back, and he explained his advertising a bit. I told him where I thought he was deficient. He said, 'Well, Mr. Maas, you have to run your business and I have to run mine. Thank you for coming.' Meeting over."

Maas had managed large Cadillac and Chevrolet dealerships throughout Texas, and he says that working with Hoffman was chaotic by comparison. "When I got to BMW, I was all by myself. If Max didn't pay warranty, I had to make it work out. If he was short on parts, I made sure we had the parts to fix most anything on the car."

Chicago-area dealer Bill Knauz added BMW to his repertoire in 1971, and he concurs with Maas' assessment even though he says he had a warm relationship with Hoffman.

"He wasn't very interested in what happened after he'd sold the cars. He didn't pay you properly on parts, service, warranty work, etc.," Knauz says. "When he built his building in Montvale, the showroom was paneled in California redwood. When we were there for the grand opening, another dealer said, 'That redwood is made out of the blood of dealers!' When it came to Max's pocket book, Max took care of Max.

"But you've got to give the devil his due. He's the guy who introduced the foreign car to the American public."

One foreign car was BMW, and of course the 2002. Dealers may have been unhappy with Max Hoffman, but they loved that car, as did their customers. If the 2002 succeeded, it was on the strength of the car itself, and because dedicated dealers like Maas, Knauz, and others soldiered on despite the difficulty of poor distributorship.

As he had regarding BMW's European distributors, Lutz became convinced that Hoffman needed to go, but his predecessor had ensured that getting rid of him would be extremely difficult. In 1970, as we've already learned, Hahnemann had signed one last contract with Hoffman before he was dismissed from the board.

This agreement, Lutz noted, was "highly unusual, to say the least." The contract ran for 12 years, then renewed automatically for another six if Hoffman built a "suitable import center in New Jersey." Also unusual was the removal, on Hoffman's request, of a normal provision stating that the franchise remained the property of the factory and could not be sold without approval.

As Lutz noted later, "The contract was signed over the protest of the legal department and [BMW AG] export manager Hermann Winkler."

In early 1972, Lutz made his first moves to resolve the situation. He established BMW of North America in New York City to deal with regulatory matters between the federal government and BMW, and to give its Munich executives a home base in the US.

Led by former GM executive (and BMW enthusiast) John Plant, the office was also hoping to help Hoffman modernize the business, and to increase sales volume and customer satisfaction through closer relations between headquarters, Hoffman Motors, and its dealers. In 1971, BMW had investigated the dealer network and found its retailers extremely poorly informed about the product; two years later, another assessment revealed no improvement, which BMW felt threatened its entire US operation.

"[Hoffman] did no believe in dealer meetings," Lutz said. "I said, 'Maxie, we've got to have a dealer meeting, generate some enthusiasm, outline our marketing plan…'

"He said, 'Bob, let me tell you. You never want to get all the dealers in one room. That's one of the rules. Because then they start comparing notes, and then they figure out that I do things for some of them that I don't do for others.'

"I said, 'Well, you can't run a national distribution system by playing favorites.' He basically said, 'It works for me and I'm not going to change it.'"

Hoffman's intransigence led BMW to initiate legal measures to extricate itself from the contract in April 1972. One of the company's US lawyers, George Galland, was a BMW owner and driver, and his notes (in the BMW Archive) provide anecdotal information about his experiences as such.

"The mechanic who services my BMW tells me that while Hoffman gives fairly good service on fast-selling items, this is not true of parts for which the demand is less heavy, the result being that some BMW cars are off the road for weeks or months," Galland wrote to BMW export manager Winkler. "My mechanic reports that Hoffman is unobliging in giving out information as to maintenance problems. Seriously harmful to BMW's interests.

"Cars aren't prepped properly. Each of two Bavarias I drove had defects. Windshield wipers inoperative, faulty mechanism for holding the hood up, carpeting unglued."

Galland's 2002 had problems, too. When its air pump broke, Hoffman refused to fix it under warranty. "Mine was not a unique experience," Galland wrote.

Naturally, Hoffman fought to keep his distributorship, trying to bribe Lutz into working with him—under a similar arrangement, presumably, to what he'd had with Hahnemann.

"He repeatedly asked me, 'How much do you make?' I'd say, 'None of your business, Maxie.'

"'No, no, I want to know. You're a nice young man. You're very smart. I want to see you do well. I don't think they're paying you enough.'"

"I said, 'Believe me, Maxie, I'm very satisfied with my financial arrangements.'

"He said, 'Ah, but I could make you so rich. If you'd cooperate with me, I could make you so rich.'"

Lutz's notes from February 12, 1973 report that Hoffman "somewhat ambiguously offered me $3,000,000 worth of HMC shares in exchange for our full cooperation, which Hoffman compared to the modest size of my annual compensation. At best it was unclear whether the offer was being made to BMW or to me personally. After forcing clarity on this point, I indicated that BMW would only be interested if the $3 million represented a significant portion of the equity, and if this were to pave the way for a larger acquisition by our company, culminating in control upon Hoffman's death or retirement. Hoffman answered very negatively and evasively, and further discussion proved fruitless."

Lutz told *Bimmer* that his refusal to be bribed prompted Hoffman to suggest that his Italian customers might be unhappy to see Hoffman Motors go out of business. "'They really like me, and it would be so unfortunate if something were to happen to you,'" Lutz said, imitating Hoffman's Viennese accent. "It was like a bad movie."

In the meantime, Lutz and Plant attempted to impose conventional business practices on BMW's US operations, including spare parts inventories. In February 1974, Plant noted, "Mr. Hoffman stated that his parts business was unprofitable and that perhaps BMW should like

Bob Lutz in his office at BMW in 1974.

to take over this function. Later on, when Mr. Lutz suggested that BMW formulate an offer, Mr. Hoffman quickly backed out and indicated that the comment had only been facetious."

It wasn't the only instance in which Hoffman changed his mind. On April 29, 1974, Lutz (plus von Kuenheim, Winkler, Plant, and several other BMW AG executives) met with Hoffman at the Pierre Hotel in New York to develop a system for streamlining the ordering and distribution process, which had stalled when Hoffman refused to accept an allotment of cars. The next day, von Kuenheim and Hoffman met alone, with von Kuenheim reporting that Hoffman agreed to consider a financial collaboration, as well as to accept all unshipped cars from the January through March allotment, the cars he'd ordered for June, and additional model year 1974 vehicles from July production.

Two days later, in a meeting with Plant and other BMW AG executives, Hoffman reneged.

"To our astonishment," Plant wrote, "Mr. Hoffman not only expressed his unwillingness to accept 1974 models from July production, but also threatened not to take unshipped units and to cancel June orders. The ensuing argument lasted the remainder of the workday.

"We repeatedly reminded them that it was not our intention to stuff them with cars. In fact, we frequently suggested that their position could best be substantiated by a joint review of their proposed retail forecast. They were

Works council representative Kurt Golda (left) confers with Herbert Quandt. Despite their differences in background, the two had a strong relationship and cooperated closely for decades.

resolutely unwilling to cooperate in working out or even discussing any forward sales projections with us."

"Their position of total non-cooperation represented a total retreat from the agreement reached with Mr. von Kuenheim two days prior. We made no demands regarding orders for production but merely attempted to arrive at a retail forecast as a basis of planning an orderly model cleanup."

Customer demand for BMW's automobiles—particularly the 2002—still outstripped supply in the US, making Hoffman's refusal to accept cars baffling. Was cash flow a problem? Plant's notes also indicate that Hoffman had several outstanding invoices with BMW, about which Hoffman insisted upon speaking to Plant alone, unaccompanied by other representatives from BMW in Munich. Plant refused, insisting that the discussion concerned all of the assembled executives.

Meanwhile, Hoffman's unpredictable ordering process was creating problems for BMW on the factory floor, which were conveyed to Herbert Quandt by BMW works council representative Kurt Golda. Golda told Quandt that the "relationship with Hoffman left employees not just disappointed but bitter. Hoffman's low numbers and erratic ordering led to layoffs, part-time work, and insecurity for the workers."

Quandt in turn pressed von Kuenheim to deal with the "burdens that now arise from the contract with Hoffman."

Hoffman claimed that BMW's attempts to influence his business practices amounted to "harassment." He told BMW executives that the company's attempts to take over its US operation would be countered by his "excellent lawyers," who believed that Hoffman's business was protected by US laws regarding automotive franchises.

On July 9, 1974, BMW terminated its contract with Hoffman for "serious commercial reasons." The company attempted to create a joint distribution company in which it held 51%, but Hoffman broke off negotiations and sued BMW that September. BMW countersued in Munich and in US federal court, citing the damaging nature of Hoffman's business practices.

In March 1975, the parties reached a settlement. Hoffman didn't get the $60 million at which he valued his import franchise, but he did get more than $35 million. In addition, he'd collect a fee of several hundred dollars for every BMW sold in the US through 1986, which amounted to millions per year, and he retained the right to consult with BMW regarding design issues for North America. In addition, BMW NA was required to lease Hoffman's headquarters and distribution facilities in New Jersey, Los Angeles, and other locations.

In 1981, six years after losing the last of his import businesses, Hoffman died at age 77. In 1982, his wife Marion created the Maximilian E. and Marion O. Hoffman Foundation. Marion died in 1983, and the couple had no children. The Hoffman Foundation has a current endowment of around $55-60 million, from which it provides grants to education, health and children's organizations, mostly in Connecticut.

The BMW 2002 is practical, roomy and economical. But in spite of all that it isn't boring.

Most cars simply are not built to perform in such a way that driving becomes an end — not merely a means of getting somewhere.

The BMW, on the other hand, is.

If a single generalization could be made to describe all BMW automobiles, it would be that each is a unique combination not only of the refined luxury you'd expect in a costly European car, but also of the extraordinary performance you'd expect only in a sports car.

What is it that makes a car so impressive that — for six years running — the readers of Car & Driver magazine vote it "The Best Sports Sedan in the World"?

Technically, the 2002 is a combination of an exceptionally responsive 2-liter engine, legendary suspension, unusually reliable performance, innovative safety features, efficient use of fuel and practical use of space.

But, in truth, the 2002 is as much a product of a state of mind about building cars as the certain way it performs.

In an age of mass-produced status symbols, marketing geniuses and styling breakthroughs, the engineers at BMW concentrate on building the best driving machines it is physically and technically possible to build.

If the thought of owning such a car intrigues you, we suggest you acquaint yourself with your BMW dealer. And make an appointment for a test drive.

The ultimate driving machine.

Bavarian Motor Works, Munich, Germany.

© 1975 BMW of North America, Inc.
Montvale, N.J. 07645 and 12541 Beatrice St., Los Angeles, Calif. 90066. Contact your nearest BMW dealer for further information. Convenient overseas delivery plan available.

In the end, a new beginning

Having settled with Hoffman, BMW of North America became the official sales and marketing arm of Bavarian Motor Works in the US. It was BMW's fourth wholly-owned sales subsidiary, following France, Belgium and Italy, and it formed a crucial piece of the puzzle in helping BMW AG gain control over not just its overseas profits but also its presentation in foreign markets.

"One of the first things I knew we had to do was hire an advertising agency to handle the BMW brand in North America," Bob Lutz told *Bimmer* magazine's Marty Bernstein in 2013.

Lutz conducted an agency review, after which BMW hired Ammirati & Puris to create a new campaign that would launch as soon as BMW of North America took over from Hoffman. Visually, the ads from Ammirati & Puris represented a continuation of those devised by James Neal Harvey, updated with sans serif type but otherwise retaining the same format.

The real departure lay in a new tagline written by agency principal Martin Puris, which dubbed BMW "The ultimate driving machine."

"I think we were the only agency that understood the car," Puris told Bernstein.

Indeed, the tagline expressed what enthusiasts had known all along, capturing the essence of BMW for both the cognoscenti and those encountering the brand for the very first time. It also came to define BMW *to itself*, giving the marque a standard against which its cars could be measured.

Ammirati & Puris had been engaged in anticipation of a settlement with Hoffman, but BMW of North America couldn't advertise until it became the importer of record in the US. It could, however, bring BMW Motorsport and its CSLs from Munich to the US, where they could garner favorable publicity by racing in the North American IMSA GT series. The new company could also support the Miller & Norburn team that was racing a 2002 with great success in IMSA Racing Stock (RS), a support class to GT.

By the time a Motorsport CSL won at Sebring on March 21, Hoffman had been deposed, and BMW NA was able to celebrate with ads touting the CSL as "the ultimate driving machine." At the end of the season, it did so again when Nick Craw and the Miller & Norburn 2002 won the IMSA RS championship, creating still more visibility for the new sales subsidiary.

The IMSA RS class had been created to rival the SCCA Trans-Am, and it followed much the same formula. Requiring nearly stock cars and parts, it rewarded the kind of native hot-rodding that engineer Preston Miller had mastered in North Carolina.

"When you raced BMWs in those classes, none of the factory racing parts were legal," says Miller. "We even had to start with a single-barrel carburetor! I had American pistons made, American cams… We had to be very inventive, and I had an elaborate dyno system for evaluating engines, which is why our engine failure rate was so low. There wasn't much we could do with the chassis. You couldn't lower the car—it had to be just as it came off the street. We fudged a little with tii parts, but we had to make production parts work."

Along with Miller's expertise, Miller & Norburn had a secret weapon in driver Nick Craw, a Princeton graduate who'd resigned as director of the Peace Corps to race full-time. Driving the M&N 2002 from 1973 to 1975, Craw won more races than any other driver in the series. He ended the 1973 season as Class B co-champion with AMC Gremlin driver Amos Johnson, to whom he lost the '74 title at the last race of the year before coming back to win the Class B title outright in 1975. (Craw also had

to beat fellow 2002 driver Ray Korman, back in the US after racing and winning with a BMW-sponsored 1800 in Asia.)

Like Trans-Am racer Don Pike, Craw praised the 2002's chassis. Unlike Pike, he had no complaints about his engines.

"What made the car effective on the track was its handling and a reliable power band. We had only one engine failure, and it was my fault, not the car's," Craw says. "And what we lost on the super-speedways we more than made up on the road courses."

By the time BMW of North America was advertising those IMSA victories, the man who'd created the new sales subsidiary and BMW Motorsport was gone. Although his initial contract had been renewed by Herbert Quandt, Bob Lutz left BMW for Ford on July 31, 1974. In two and a half years, he'd left an indelible mark on BMW, but managerial friction with von Kuenheim over cars like the 2002 turbo and the Batmobile CSL strained the relationship.

"We had our disagreements, but we were good friends," Lutz said. "Years later, he would say to me, 'You probably saved BMW with your initiative of eliminating European distributors and replacing them with national sales companies, because that was the real swing to profitability.'"

Indeed it was. From 1974 to 1979, BMW AG's annual net profits more than doubled, from DM 42 million to 100 million. Profits from US exports were critical, especially after sales spiked following the takeover from Hoffman.

In March 1975, BMW NA's first CEO Jack Cook met the US press for the first time, announcing that BMW hoped to sell 18,000 cars in the US that year. By the end of 1975, BMW had exported a record 21,057 cars to the US, exceeding Cook's prediction handily.

Of those, 15,712 were 2002s, which defied the usual trajectory when the model had its best year ever in its eighth year on the market. That figure is even more remarkable when one considers that imports were reduced to a trickle in the first three months of the year, while negotiations between Hoffman and BMW were taking place.

Attesting even further to the 2002's enduring popularity—and its unmet potential during the Hoffman era—that record was set with only a single model, not several. By 1975, BMW offered only the carbureted 2002 in the US.

Production of the E21 3 Series had begun in Munich in July of that year, but the older E10 continued to be built alongside it while the E21 was certified for compliance with US safety and emissions standards.

Despite anticipation for the new 3 Series, the 2002 continued to sell strongly. In the first seven months of 1976, BMW exported 9,634 examples of its venerable 2002 before the E21 took over in August. Had the 2002 been available all year, sales might have exceeded 16,000 units in 1976.

The body style continued to appeal to customers in Europe, too, where BMW offered the 75-hp 1502 to customers priced out of the initial 3 Series offering. It proved highly popular, with nearly 71,000 examples built over three years. All told, BMW produced 837,335 Type 114s in its Milbertshofen plant, plus another 13,530 from complete knock-down (CKD) kits sent to Portugal and Uruguay for assembly.

BMW had exported 112,520 of its Munich-built Type 114/E10s to the US between 1967 and 1976—13% of total production, to a market where BMW had been virtually unknown prior to the car's arrival. Of those, 99,538 were 2002s, while 13,162 were 1600-2/1602s.

More important than the numbers, the 2002 made a deep impression on a generation of enthusiasts, to whom it introduced BMW's unique combination of sporty performance, practicality, and reliability.

The E21 and subsequent 3 Series took BMW to new heights, but the success of those models rested on the foundation created by its predecessor. Enthusiasts have long recognized the 2002's importance to BMW, and they've been celebrating the model at festivals worldwide since the turn of the century. They're also willing to pay real money to get one: A solid example commands around ten times its price when new, and the best examples—especially the rare turbos—can bring six-figure prices at auction.

Within BMW, the 2002 continues to reverberate as a touchstone for the company's designers, engineers, and executives.

In 2005, BMW Mobile Tradition (now Classic) built an all-new 2002 from an unused body shell to demonstrate the availability of all the spare parts needed to keep a vintage 2002 on the road.

In 2007, BMW revealed its Concept 1 Series tii, a performance version of the 1 Series Coupe, at the Tokyo Motor Show. BMW board member Stefan Krause said the car "continues our legacy of small, sporty coupes, and shows BMW's classical brand values in a very fresh, passionate fashion." The concept didn't have much in common with a 2002 tii beyond its name, but it followed the tii formula of high performance and relatively light weight.

In 2011, when the Concept tii reached production as the 1 Series M Coupe, it was billed as the 2002 tii's spiritual successor. Television ads showed the 1M Coupe running alongside a 2002 tii, and BMW NA placed the two cars side by side at the New York auto show, lest any doubt remain about the 1M's lineage.

In 2016, fifty years after the Type 114's debut, BMW Design created the 2002 Hommage. A retro-styled sports coupe built atop the M2 platform, it drew upon the legacy of the 2002 turbo. At Villa d'Este, the Hommage debuted in traditional Motorsport stripes atop vintage Fjord blue metallic paint. At Monterey, that livery was swapped for Alpina-esque orange and black, with "Turbomeister" graphics recalling the Jägermeister logos on so many 1970s BMW race cars.

Automotive technology has moved on, but the 2002 remains the quintessential BMW, now and forever.

Appendix: BMW's Type 114 exports to the US, 1966-1976

Year	1600-2 exports	2002 exports	Total BMW exports
1966	355 *(Includes some New Class 1600 sedans)*		1,253
1967	4,362		4,564
1968	5,236	3,892	9,172
1969	2,675	6,962	11,638
1970	1,375	6,667	10,029
1971	701	9,010	13,560
1972	1	9,360	15,113
1973		8,962	13,789
1974	2	13,959	19,636
1975		16,712	21,057
1976		9,634	26,061

Bibliography

While much of what is written herein is based on original research done in Munich at the BMW Archive or in interviews with persons having first-hand knowledge of events, the following books and articles also provided valuable information:

The BMW Story: A company in its time, by Horst Mönnich. 1991, Sidgwick & Jackson LTD, London, England.

BMW 2002: The cult car, by Walter Zeichner. 1998, BMW Mobile Tradition, Munich, Germany.

BMW, Bavaria's Driving Machines, by Jan P. Norbye. 1984, Beekman House, New York, New York.

The legendary BMW 507, by Dr. Karlheinz Lange. 2005, BMW Mobile Tradition, Munich, Germany.

BMW 328: From roadster to legend, by Rainer Simons. 1996, BMW Mobile Tradition, Munich, Germany.

BMW Since 1916, by Manfred Grunert and Florian Triebel. 2006, BMW Mobile Tradition, Munich, Germany.

The BMW home plant in Munich, by Caroline Schulenburg and Andreas Hemmerle. 2007, BMW Mobile Tradition, Munich, Germany.

BMW Engines, 1916-2000, by Dr. Karlheinz Lange. 1999, BMW Mobile Tradition, Munich, Germany.

Die Inernationalizierung der Bayerische Motoren Werke AG, by Annika Biss. 2017, Walter de Gruyter GmbH, Berlin/Boston.

BMW, A History, by Halwart Schrader and Ron Wakefield. 1979, Princeton Publishing, Princeton, New Jersey.

"Max Hoffman and the North American Automobie Market," by Sasha Schindler. 2015, Philosophische Fakultät der Rheinischen Friedrich-Wilhelms-Universität Bonn.

"The Baron of Park Avenue," by Karl Ludvigsen. *Automobile Quarterly*, Vol. 10, No. 2, 1972.

"Motor Man Max," by Karl Ludvigsen. *Bimmer*, April 1998.

"The ultimate ad slogan," by Marty Bernstein. *Bimmer*, February 2014.

"The Amazing Max Hoffman," by Marty Bernstein and Jackie Jouret. *Bimmer*, August 2014.

"An Iconoclast in Munich," by Bill Cobb. *Bimmer*, October 2016.

Some of the material in this book was published in *The ICON: 50 Years of the BMW 2002*, by Jackie Jouret, BMW CCA Foundation, 2018.

Acknowledgements

This book would not have been possible without the cooperation of the BMW Archive, where I was allowed to examine countless original documents related to the creation of the 2002 and BMW's relationship with Max Hoffman. Thanks to the Archive's Manfred Grunert, Stefan Behr, Dr. Annika Biss, Fred Jakobs, Marc Thiesbürger, Andreas Harz, and Ruth Standfuss for their help in locating and interpreting these documents, and for providing the accompanying photos. Thanks, too, to Sasha Schindler, whose Master's thesis on Max Hoffman's relationship with Mercedes-Benz and BMW provided valuable information and pointed me toward specific documents within the Archive that I might not have found on my own.

Thanks to Paul Bracq and David Carp for illuminating the design process of the 2002 and its variants. Thanks to Karl Ludvigsen for interviewing Max Hoffman while Hoffman was still alive, and for putting up with my inquiries for additional information as I attempted to wrestle with Hoffman's legacy at BMW. Thanks to Marty Bernstein and Bill Cobb, who interviewed Bob Lutz for *Bimmer* magazine during my tenure as editor, asking questions on my behalf and providing me with crucial direction for further investigation into the Hoffman era.

Thanks to Joseph Chamberlain, Michael Izor, Rob Mitchell, Preston Miller, Peter Brock, Mike Self, and everyone else within the 2002 community who talked to me about the early days of the 2002 in the US, and who brought the era to life with their stories.

Thanks, as always, to Tom Plucinsky and everyone in the corporate communications department at BMW of North America, past and present. You have always been supremely helpful and enthusiastic.

—*Jackie Jouret*
Portland, Oregon 2019

Author photo by Helmut Werb

Index of characters

Aaltonen, Rauno 74
Baur, Karl 68, 70, 71
Bein, Helmut 74
Bernstein, Marty 42, 121
Bertram, Georg 21, 25, 26, 28, 80-83, 93
Biss, Dr. Annika 43, 50
Böning, Alfred 13, 15-16
Bönsch, Helmut-Werner 16, 47, 49, 51
Bovensiepen, Burkard 49, 51, 65
Bracq, Paul 68-69, 79, 82, 84, 93, 94, 105-106, 108
Brecht, Tim 64
Brock, Peter 64, 122

Carp, David 67, 80, 82
Castiglioni, Camilo 11
Chamberlain, Joseph 62
Charbonneaux, Philippe 69
Chinetti, Luigi 113
Cobb, Bill 38
Cook, Jack 123
Craig, Jim 62
Craw, Nick 122-123
Cunningham, Rug 64

Davenport, John 74
Davis, Jr., David E. 45, 49-51, 58-59, 61-62
Denzel, Wolfgang 17
Dietrich, Marlene 50
Donath, Kurt 23
Dye, Glen 47-50

Ewell, John 14

Falkenhausen, Alexander von 19-21, 28, 45-47, 49, 51, 74, 104
Fiedler, Fritz 12-13, 19
Fredericks, Carl Jr. 63-64
Frére, Paul 106-109
Friz, Max 12
Frua, Pietro 31, 80-82

Galland, George 116
Gandini, Marcelo 93-94
Gieschen, Wilhelm 23, 28, 50
Glas, Andreas 32

Glas, Hans 80
Goertz, Albrecht von 39-40
Golda, Kurt 118
Grewenig, Hanns 15-16, 23

Hack, Gert 66
Hahne, Hubert 47, 64-65
Hahnemann, Paul 23-28, 32, 42-43, 46-47, 50-51, 60, 68, 71, 79, 92, 112-116
Harvey, James Neal 34, 54-55, 77, 114, 121
Henne, Ernst 12-14, 31
Hitler, Adolf 14
Hof, Ernst 16, 23, 40
Hoffman, Marion 119
Hoffman, Max 9, 33-34, 36-38, 41, 57, 59-60, 62-63, 77, 83-84, 111-119, 121-123
Hofmeister, Wilhelm 19, 21, 67, 82, 93

Izor, Michael 61

Jakobs, Fred 43
Johnson, Amos 123

Kämpfer, Ernst 23
Knauz, Bill 115
Koch, Hans 92
Kolk, Oscar 24
Korman, Ray 123
Kuenheim, Eberhard von 91-92, 94, 105, 111, 118-119, 123

Lamm, Charly 65
Lange, Dr. Karlheinz 41, 74
Loof, Ernst 39
Ludvigsen, Karl 38, 41, 42, 113
Lutz, Bob 38-39, 91-93, 94, 101, 103-106, 110-111, 114-115, 117, 121, 123
Lyons, William 93

Maas, Lee 115
Mandel, Leon 61
Mehrman, Bob 62
Mehmel, Hans-Christoph 74
Meier, Schorsch 32, 43
Michelotti, Giovanni 17, 25-26, 81-82
Miller, Nels 64
Miller, Preston 122-123
Mitchell, Bill 106

Mitchell, Rob 61-62
Mönnich, Horst 24, 113
Monz, Karl 23, 92
Müller, Max 91

Nixon, Richard 75

Oppenheimer, Fred 40-42, 112
Osswald, Bernhard 50, 52, 54, 92

Pike, Don 64, 123
Plant, John 116-120
Pleasant, Mickey 64
Popp, Franz Josef 12
Potheau, Michel 62

Quandt, Gunther 18
Quandt, Harald 18, 91
Quandt, Herbert 17-19, 22-24, 26, 32, 91, 94, 113, 118-119, 123
Quester, Dieter 64, 65, 104

Rech, Karl 12, 20, 45
Rennen, Manfred 21, 80-84, 93-94
Richter-Brohm, Heinrich 16-17, 23, 41, 113
Rosche, Paul 104-105

Scilley, Roger 62
Schleicher, Rudolf 12-14, 19-20
Schuster, Peter 63
Schnitzer, Josef and Herbert 65, 103-104
Shirachi, Doug 62
Sonne, Karl-Heinz 26-27, 47, 113
Szimanowski, Peter 16, 21

Theobald, Nell 33

Walker, Steve 64
Warmbold, Achim 74
Wenzelburger, Hermann 69-70
Wilcke, Gerhard 47, 51, 113-114
Winkler, Hermann 116-117
Wolff, Eberhard 19, 21

Yates, Brock 61

Zasada, Sobieslaw 74
Ziereis, Hans 63

www.ingramcontent.com/pod-product-compliance
Lightning Source LLC
Chambersburg PA
CBHW082126230426
43671CB00015B/2818